CONTRIBUTING WRITERS

Our thanks to the following persons who contributed to the writing of these Bible Study Guides.

Delores Johnson, Marion Love, Karen McClelland, Lynn Oliver, Richard Simmons, Alice Standback, and Vanessa Wilbourn.

Publisher
Urban Ministries, Inc.
P.O. Box 463987
Chicago, IL 60643-6987

ISBN: 0-940955-38-5
Catalog #: 1-11

Scripture Quotations
Unless otherwise noted, Scripture texts are taken from the King James Version of the Bible.

TABLE OF CONTENTS

Preface

How To Use This Book

The materials in these studies provide for in-depth exploration of the Scriptures. At the same time we recognize that merely studying Bible texts as an end in itself is not adequate to accomplish all that should be accomplished. The Scriptures make clear that God's purpose for people is that first they would come to know Him as Saviour (2 Peter 3:9), then go on to develop their relationship with Him so their lifestyles increasingly reflect the character of Jesus Christ (1 Peter 2:2).

We read in Romans 8:29 that God "predestinated [us] to be conformed to the image of His Son..." In other words, God's desires for believers is that they become more and more like Jesus Christ in character. We know that Jesus Christ is perfect and that we will never reach ultimate perfection in this lifetime. At the same time we are encouraged to pursue the likeness of Christ. Note the purpose of each of the following sections which appear throughout the studies:

DEFINING THE ISSUE, AIM SCRIPTURE TEXT, BIBLE BACKGROUND, POINTS TO PONDER, GOD'S TRUTH-AT-A-GLANCE, EXPLORING THE MEANING, DISCERNING MY DUTY, DECIDING MY RESPONSE, WHAT I WILL DO, and LIGHT ON THE HEAVY.

DEFINING THE ISSUE

These studies are designed to help people grow in their relationship with Jesus Christ, to foster discipleship. Each study begins with a section we call "DEFINING THE ISSUE." The purpose of this is to elevate a life need which will be addressed in the exploration of the Scripture text.

Scholars have observed that every book in the Bible was written to address a life need which the people to whom the book is address were experiencing, whether to document their history, deal with a false doctrine, or encourage holiness of life.

AIM

This is a statement of what the study is designed to accomplish in the life of the participant. Such aims can be modified to address the needs which the leader of the group senses to be those of the group. A leader should never feel that the written aim has be slavishly adhered to. The study is a "guide," not an unchangeable focus.

SCRIPTURE TEXT

This section includes a printed portion of Scripture upon which the study focuses. While the studies were prepared using the King James Version of the Bible, any version which the group prefers can be used. This section begins with an outline of the text which facilitates dividing the Scripture into smaller segments.

BIBLE BACKGROUND

Provides contextual material which can aid in understanding the people to whom the Scripture was originally addressed. It also explains the context for the Scripture portion so the text is easier to grasp.

POINTS TO PONDER

These questions are designed to help focus the minds of participants on some of the areas the study will address and to facilitate understanding the text.

DISCUSSING THE MEANING

Comments on the Scripture texts will be found in this section. If at all possible, participants will have read this material prior to the gathering so that reading entire sections is not necessary. However, the leader may want portions to be read in order to reinforce a particular point of discussion.

DISCERNING MY DUTY

Since the discussion of meaning should not be an end in itself, we have provided a section entitled, "DISCERNING MY DUTY." While in many cases this allows the participant to think about individual responses to the Scripture, occasionally this exercise may focus on group action. This is especially helpful if you think of your group as more than a "study" group. That is, your people will occasionally want to collectively engage in some activity which reinforces the aim of the study and, at the same time, promote the welfare of others.

DECIDING MY RESPONSE
Since there is a difference between know that could be done and actually doing it, "DECIDING MY RESPONSE" allows a participant to pinpoint what their response will be as a result of discovering what could be done.

WHAT I WILL DO
The section entitled, "WHAT I WILL DO," is to allow the participant to make a note of any action he/she will take after the study is completed.

We believe this approach to the study of Scripture will not only be exciting to all the participants, but will result in real spiritual growth—discipleship.

LIGHT ON THE HEAVY
This section will provide additional information on a word or theme deemed with may be helpful to the readers.

OTHER SUGGESTIONS
1. *As a way of strengthening the bonds among people within your group, you may want to plan some kind of social event once per quarter. This may consist of a potluck supper, a dinner/outing, etc.*

2. *You may want to consider some form of ministry activity during the course of a study such as one of the following.*
   —Conduct a jail or prison service.
   —Make or purchase gifts for public or private school class.
   —Organize a special church cleaning.
   —Conduct a fundraising project for a missionary.

—*Gather clothing for needy children.*

—*Write letters to a politician on a local or national issue of morality or justice.*

—*Fundraiser to send a need child to a summer camp or vacation.*

A little time spent brainstorming in your group will produce lots of other ideas for serving the Lord and people in a practical way.

3. *You may want to use a portion of your time to allow your group members to pray for one another and for needs of the church.*

Introduction

THE AFRICAN ROOTS OF CHRISTIANITY

When we speak of African roots we are defining Africa not merely as the area from the River of Africa southward. Rather we refer to the land which extends from South Africa into Mesopotamia—present day Iraq and Iran. The tendency to isolate Mesopotamia as though it were not a part of Africa is of recent origin. Ancient peoples recognized the cultural and geographical "connectedness" of these peoples.

The location of the Garden of Eden is today more likely identified with East Africa along the Nile River because the oldest remains of human life have been found in the area near Tanzania. In the past Mesopotamia was the best choice because of the two identifiable rivers mentioned in Genesis 2, the Hiddekel and Euphrates Rivers.

It is now believed that humankind migrated from East Africa northward along the Nile into the area known as Mesopotamia then further north, east, and west. This migration from Africa into Mesopotamia is bolstered by the findings of Sir Henry Rawlinson, a noted Assyriologist. He concluded that the Sumerian culture, the earliest to exist in Mesopotamia, was brought to the area by people who came from Africa. His conclusion confirms the biblical indication that Cush, whose name means "black," was the father of Nimrod. Nimrod built Asshur which is in Mesopotamia. It is the conclusion of many scholars that the Hamitic and Semitic people of this area were people of color. This conclusion is based upon geography, anthropology, and archaeology.

From this Land of the Chaldeans (Mesopotamia) Abraham departed around 2,000 B.C. and migrated into the land of Canaan (Genesis 12:5). When he arrived in this land he lived among other descendants of Ham through Canaan: the Sidonians, Hittites, Jebusites, Amorites, Girgasites, Hivites, Arkites, Sinites, Arvadites, Zemarites, and Hamathites (Genesis 10:15-18). The name "Ham" means "black" or "swarthy" It follows that the Canaanites, Ham's children, were people of color.

Abraham fathered Isaac, Isaac fathered Jacob and Esau, Jacob fathered 12 sons who migrated to Egypt around 1800 B.C. When they arrived in Egypt they lived among people who were black. The name "Egypt" is a Greek word which means "black." Europeans have attempted to show that the name refers only to the black soil found in the area. Other scholars have shown that the name referred to the people as well as the soil. Prior to the arrival of Greeks into that area around 332 B.C., the people called themselves "Kemet."

While in Egypt the Israelites learned much from the people among whom they lived for some 400 years. They absorbed Egyptian customs and culture, as well as learned and benefited from Egyptian education and skills. When they left the country a "mixed multitude" went with them. Bishop Alfred Dunston in his seminal work, *The Black Man in the Old Testament and Its World*, has demonstrated that this "mixed multitude" had to have been Egyptians who left with the Israelites.

When they arrived back into the land of Canaan the people of color were still there. God empowered the Israelites to break the backs of the Canaanites militarily, but they did not wipe them out. Instead they lived among, intermarried with them, and worshiped their idols (See Judges 1—3; Ezra 9).

The presence of Europeans in Egypt and Palestine did not occur until Alexander invaded Egypt in 332 B.C. When this conqueror arrived in Egypt, he was so impressed with the knowledge of Egyptians that he built the city of Alexandria where housed untold thousands of books and scrolls. African scholars have demonstrated that much of the knowledge which Greeks disseminated to the rest of the world as though it were their own, was in fact, learned from ancient Egyptians. The Romans conquered the Mediterranean world during the first century B.C. and remained there until the time of Christ. They maintained military control of the Egyptian/Mesopotamia corridor, but the complexion of the bulk of the people did not change significantly.

As the Gospel traveled out from Jerusalem, Judea, Samaria, and the utmost parts of the earth (Acts 1:8) it reached people of African descent. Those gathered at Jerusalem for Pentecost when the Holy Spirit arrived were from many countries with known African populations, including Medes, Mesopotamia, Egypt, Libya, and Cyrene.

The Ethiopian eunuch (Acts 8) was the first known non-Jew to embrace the faith (eunuchs could not be proselytes). The church at Antioch embraced mixed leadership including Simeon known as "the Black Man" (Niger). See Acts 13:1. As the Gospel reached Asia and Europe it found there Africans who had migrated into these areas. One scholarly suggestion is that the Gospel of Mark was written for the believers who lived in Cyrene where the population was Jewish in part, but overwhelmingly Black.

This discussion of the presence of Africans in the biblical record is not intended to elevate Blacks above the presence of other racial groups. Indeed, in God's economy all primary racial groups have had a part in his plan to communicate the Gospel to the entire world. The purpose is to show that Blacks have been included, not excluded as many scholars and Bible commentators have attempted to do.

Keep Hope Alive

DEFINING THE ISSUE

The Reverend Jesse Jackson has coined the phrase "Keep Hope Alive." Jackson's philosophy is that when people have hope they have a sense of purpose in life. When people don't have hope, they lose their sense of self-worth and direction.

If you've ever been to a hospital's terminal ward, you have seen images of hopelessness. When told by a doctor, "There is nothing else we can do," many people become depressed, lose their appetite and give up on life. On the other hand, research has found that when terminally ill
people find something to live for, they fight for life and often recover from their sicknesses.

Our country's economic problems have forced many people out of jobs and into the unemployment line. Not only are some Americans bitter and confused, many are also hopeless.

Some feel they may never find economic relief for their families.

In today's lesson, the Apostle Peter encourages the Christians in Asia Minor to "keep hope alive" by looking beyond the suffering of this world to faith in God through the resurrection of Jesus Christ.

AIM

By the end of the session participants should be able to:

1. *Describe the meaning of a "living hope" in God.*
2. *Share the benefits of a lively hope with those who may not know Jesus.*

3.   Commit to working through hopeless situations in their communities to bring about hope in the lives of others.

SCRIPTURE TEXT

1 PETER 1:3 Blessed be the God and Father of our Lord Jesus Christ, which according to his abundant mercy hath begotten us again unto a lively hope by the resurrection of Jesus Christ from the dead,

4 To an inheritance incorruptible, and undefiled, and that fadeth not away, reserved in heaven for you,

5 Who are kept by the power of God through faith unto salvation ready to be revealed in the last time.

6 Wherein ye greatly rejoice, though now for a season, if need be, ye are in heaviness through manifold temptations:

7 That the trial of your faith, being much more precious than of gold that perisheth, though it be tried with fire, might be found unto praise and honour and glory at the appearing of Jesus Christ:

8 Whom having not seen, ye love; in whom, though now ye see him not, yet believing, ye rejoice with joy unspeakable and full of glory:

9 Receiving the end for your faith, even the salvation of you souls.

13 Wherefore gird up the loins of your mind, be sober, and hope to the end for the grace that is to be brought unto you at the revelation of Jesus Christ;

14 As obedient children, not fashioning yourselves according to the former lusts in your ignorance:

15 But as he which hath called you is holy, so be ye holy in all manner of conversation;

16 Because it is written, Be ye holy; for I am holy.

17 And if ye call on the Father, who without respect of persons judgeth according to every man's work, pass the time of your sojourning here in fear:

18 Forasmuch as ye know that ye were not redeemed with corruptible things, as silver and gold, from your vain conversation received by tradition from your fathers;

19 But with the precious blood of Christ, as of a lamb without blemish and without spot:

20 Who verily was foreordained before the foundation of the world, but was manifest in these last times for you,

21 Who by him do believe in God, that raised him up from the dead, and gave him glory; that your faith and hope might be in God.

BIBLE BACKGROUND

First Peter is a letter of encouragement. Peter wrote this letter during a time of severe persecution of Christians. Rome's Emperor Nero had launched a ruthless attack against all who dared to speak the name of Jesus. Christians were often forced to go underground for fear of death. Others were openly rebuked and mocked before the community. Some were even killed by wild animals. The Christian church was a target of persecution by local authorities.

Peter wrote a message of hope to these despondent and distressed Christians. The Apostle Paul is recognized as the founder of most of these churches; however, God used Peter to encourage persecuted Christians to hold to their faith in the midst of turmoil.

Peter tells these believers that God has given them the gift of a living hope through Christ.

Jesus' resurrection is the evidence that God had brought salvation to the world. With this hope, these Christians could endure hardships by looking beyond the suffering of this world to God's promise of eternal life.

POINTS TO PONDER

1. *What type of hope has God brought us into?*
2. *Describe the inheritance we have from God.*
3. *What is the testing of our faith compared to?*
4. *How has God called us to live? What has He called us to be?*
5. *Through whom have we been redeemed?*

THE LESSON AT-A-GLANCE

1. *The gift of salvation (1 Peter 1:3-6)*
2. *The testing of our faith (vv. 7-9)*
3. *The call to holy living (vv. 13-16)*
4. *The cost of redemption (vv. 17-21)*

EXPLORING THE MEANING
1. The gift of salvation (1 Peter 1:3-6)

Peter tells his audience that God has begotten them into a "lively [or living] hope" (v. 3). The word "begotten" refers to giving birth, as a woman would give birth to a child. Through God's abundant mercy, we are "born" into an everlasting hope. Our spiritual birth is not an act of flesh and blood or human nature, but by and through the Holy Spirit (see John 3:5-6).

As children of God we are heirs to His kingdom. An heir is one who is entitled to receive a portion of property or possessions by virtue of his/her relationship with the owner. Through Christ, God has adopted us to become sons and daughters of His wonderful riches.

Our inheritance is not of this world, but in heaven. Thus, we are "in" the world, but not "of" it.

Peter describes the Christian's inheritance as "imperishable and undefiled and will not fade away, reserved in heaven" (v. 4, NASB). Peter's description shows the everlasting nature of God's love toward us. This inheritance is for all who believe and trust in God. Through faith we are assured that our salvation is eternal.

Peter calls upon his listeners to look beyond their present sufferings to the joy that lies ahead.

The joys of our inheritance with God greatly outweigh the heaviness of trials and tribulations in this world. Peter is not telling us to forget about the present in favor of the future. His rationale is that "our light affliction, which is but for a moment, is working for us a far more exceeding and eternal weight of glory" (2 Corinthians 4:17, NKJV).

2. The testing of our faith (vv. 7-9)

Peter also tells persecuted Christians that trials and tribulations can work to our good if we give them to God. Troubles and hardships test the sincerity of our faith. How we respond to life's problems testifies to who we are in Christ Jesus. God does not send persecution to His people.

However, God does allow persecutions to come upon us so that we might develop stronger faith, character and hope in Him.

Problems keep us "looking up" and dependent upon God for guidance. Furthermore, when we give our troubles to the Lord, we can witness firsthand God's power to deliver us in our time of need.

While we cannot see God, through our faith in His love we can "rejoice with joy unspeakable and full of glory" (v. 8). The secret to success in life comes when we learn how to look above and beyond the negative circumstances of life with the eyes of faith. Faith points us to God. When we see God, we see hope and can patiently wait on the promise of our inheritance which is the salvation of our souls (v. 9).

3. The call to holy living (vv. 13-16)

Peter then encourages the Christians to act out their hope in Christ by living holy lives before the world. First, he instructs his readers to "gird up the loins" of their minds. What we put in our minds is as important as what we put in our bodies. A mind that consistently focuses on God is kept in perfect peace (Isaiah 26:3). Next, we are to be "sober" and free from negative influences that only seek to make us unholy in the sight of God. Whom we associate with does have an influence upon our thinking and actions. Finally, Peter encourages these believers to "hope to the end for the grace that is to be brought unto you at the revelation of Jesus Christ" (v. 13). This hope "maketh [us] not ashamed, because the love of God [has been] shed abroad in our hearts by the Holy Ghost" (Romans 5:5).

Peter also encourages these believers not to slip back into their old ways of sin. Christians are not exempt from life's temptations. Despite our desire to live holy lives, we are yet mortal creatures. Peter uses the word "ignorance" (v. 14) to explain why many Christians disobey God.

Often our past sins were not based on an arrogant attitude toward the Lord, but on the lack of knowledge about God's love for us. Many people have a zeal for God, but not according to the truth of His Word. People usually do better when they know better.

God calls us to be holy. The word "holy" refers to a person being separated to do the things of God. We are to be holy because "He who hath called us is holy" (v. 15a). The holiness of God requires that those who follow Him seek to live holy. This holy living must be in "all . . .behavior" (15b, NASB). Christians are salt and light in the world. God calls us to let our lights shine in such a way that people will desire to walk like us and glorify our heavenly Father (see Matthew 5:16).

4. The cost of redemption (vv. 17-21)

Peter urges his listeners to conduct themselves in fear of the Lord. This doesn't mean we are to cower in a corner trying to hide from God. Rather, we are to pay reverence to God for who He is and conduct ourselves in a way that shows the importance of respecting and honoring our heavenly Father in every way.

Next Peter reminds the church that while God's grace is free, it is not cheap. We were redeemed or purchased not with corruptible things like silver and gold, but with the precious blood of Christ (v. 19). Because of Jesus' shed blood, we are no longer under the bondage of sin and the law. Jesus came as the sacrificial lamb without blemish and spot to take away the sins of the world.

God foreknew and foreordained this divine plan of salvation. The Lord knew we would rebel and turn our face from Him. Nevertheless, at the right time, God sent Jesus to save the world.

But God commandeth His love toward us in that, while we were yet sinners, "Christ died for us'" (Romans 5:8). Through the power of God, who has raised Jesus from the dead, we now have hope in God.

This free gift of God is our reason to praise and hope in the Father's love. God has done for us what we could not do for ourselves. The cross is the visible evidence that God cares for us. The empty tomb is the proof that God has completed His plan of redemption. Based on what God hasdone for us, Christians should "sanctify the Lord God in [their] hearts, and be ready always to give an answer to every man that asketh you a reason of hope that is in you" (1 Peter 3:15).

God's divine plan includes a lively hope, based on the death and resurrection of Jesus Christ and our desire to live for Him. When we recognize the power of the hope God has given us, we can be confident that He will bring us through the trials and problems of life.

DISCERNING MY DUTY

1. *What did Peter mean by a "lively" hope?*
2. *Do trials and tribulations build our faith? Explain.*
3. *Why is it important to keep our minds sober and free from negative influences?*
4. *What does it mean to be holy?*
5. *Explain what it means to be redeemed.*

DECIDING MY RESPONSE

To think about—Nobody likes to feel alone and without hope in our society. Crises and negative circumstances in life present us with situations that tempt us to give up and stop trying.

However, our hope is in Christ who never fails. How can we get this message across to the world?

To do—Meditate on what God's love through Christ means to you. Ask God to help you get the message of hope over to hopeless people. Recognize that your mission "field" begins right where you are. Pray for guidance in knowing where to go and what to do. Make the slogan "Keep Hope Alive" more than just a catch phrase. Look for opportunities in your community where hope is alive. Where hopeless situations abound, seek God's guidance in what to do.

Write out your plans and intentions and seek to work through them this week. Give a praise report next week.

WHAT I WILL DO

_____

_____

LIGHT ON THE HEAVY

Salvation—Refers to the process whereby God saves or delivers us from danger, bondage and sin. In the Old Testament, the word refers more to God's delivering power from physical danger. Anyone who brings about this deliverance or freedom from bondage is referred to as a "Saviour."

The New Testament places greater emphasis upon salvation as God's act of grace toward fallen human beings. This was expressed through the death of Jesus Christ. Through this act, God redeemed fallen humanity from their state of hopelessness. Finally, salvation is a free gift to all who ask. We are not saved by how good we are to God, but how good God is to us. (Martin, William C., *The Layman's Bible Encyclopedia:* The Southwestern Company, 1964, pp. 722-723).

Peter—A descriptive Greek name which is the name by which we best know the apostle "The Man of Rock." It must not be forgotten that this was his nickname, or "given name," bestowed upon him by Jesus (Matthew 16:18). Born Simon, under the hand of Jesus who chose him and the Holy Spirit who came to control him, the "given name" was justified, and Peter became a Rock a strong, firm character.

Born a Jew, he grew up a fisherman, and was indirectly "converted" by John the Baptist (see John 1:35-42). Although not conscious of it, Peter was destined to achieve eminence in the ranks of the One who saw great possibilities in him. At the time of his call, Peter, along with the rest of the humble fishermen of Galilee, had much to learn and unlearn before the high requirements of Christ were satisfied. As for Peter, Jesus knew he would grow in grace and in the knowledge of Himself (2 Peter 3:18).

Peter was often volatile, extreme, and forever asking questions. While he had his moments of rapture and high vision, he was also conscious of the depths of sin within his being. He was a denier and blasphemer and became an encourager. Perhaps the hardest lesson Peter had to learn from his Lord was humility (see John 13:3-10).

As an apostle Peter wrote two epistles. Ostervald says that First Peter is "one of the finest books of the New Testament." Probably written for both Jewish and Gentile converts scattered throughout Asia Minor, the letter is peculiarly characterized by energy and dignity. Scholars agree that eventually Peter died by being crucified as predicted by our Lord (see John 21:18). (*All the Apostles of the Bible.* Vol. 1, 1972, Grand Rapids Michigan: Zondervan Publishing Co., pp. 126-152).

Called to Be God's People

DEFINING THE ISSUE

One of the most popular songs in 1991 was sung by Timothy Wright entitled, "Who's on the Lord's Side?"It encouraged believers to take a stand and make it known to all just whose side they were on.

Often, we are placed in situations where we are confronted with deciding whose side we are on. Unfortunately, by our actions, we do not always display that we are on the Lord's side. We need the Holy Spirit's power and determination to let everybody know we have been called by God to be His people.

It is not always easy to be God's people. Some members in society are anti-God. Yet, despite the world's influence, we can maintain powerful testimony if we take a stand and show others that God is real because He lives in us.

In this study the Apostle Peter continues his exhortation to the suffering Christians by helping them understand the importance of being called by God and walking with God's guidance despite persecution and ridicule in the world.

AIM

Participants should by the end of the study:

1. *Describe how we are God's people.*
2. *Decide to study the Bible so they will grow on the pure milk of the Word.*
3. *Be a blessing to someone in their family and church so they can help someone grow in the knowledge of Christ.*

SCRIPTURE TEXT

1 PETER 2:1 Wherefore laying aside all malice, and all guile, and hypocrisies, and envies, and all evil speakings,

2 As newborn babes, desire the sincere milk of the word, that ye may grow thereby:

3 If so be ye have tasted that the Lord is gracious.

4 To whom coming, as unto a living stone, disallowed indeed of men, but chosen of God, and precious,

5 Ye also, as lively stones, are built up a spiritual house, an holy priesthood, to offer up spiritual sacrifices, acceptable to God by Jesus Christ.

6 Wherefore also it is contained in the scripture, Behold, I lay in Sion a chief corner stone, elect, precious: and he that believeth on him shall not be confounded.

7 Unto you therefore which believe he is precious: but unto them which be disobedient, the stone which the builders disallowed, the same is made the head of the corner,

8 And a stone of stumbling, and a rock of offence, even to them which stumble at the word, being disobedient: whereunto also they were appointed.

9 But ye are a chosen generation, a royal priesthood, an holy nation, a peculiar people; that ye should shew forth the praises of him who hath called you out of darkness into his marvellous light:

10 Which in time past were not a people, but are now the people of God: which had not obtained mercy, but now have obtained mercy.

BIBLE BACKGROUND

In the previous lesson the Apostle Peter exhorted us to live holy lives since we are begotten into a lively hope through Jesus Christ our Lord. Peter wanted people to know that they were redeemed with the precious blood of Jesus.

Peter's letter was addressed to the predominantly Gentile Christians who were scattered throughout the world and were suffering because of their faith (see 1 Peter 1:1). Though they suffered extreme persecution, Peter encouraged them to rejoice and live above hostility and threats so that the power of Christ could be revealed in their lives.

As we begin this lesson, Peter shares some foundational truths that can help his readers grow in grace and knowledge of the Lord Jesus Christ.

POINTS TO PONDER

1. *What does Peter admonish us to lay aside?*
2. *What should believers desire?*
3. *What happened when Christ was rejected by men?*
4. *To what are believers being built?*
5. *From what did God call us?*
6. *How do believers obtain mercy?*

THE LESSON AT-A-GLANCE

1. *Growing in the Lord (1 Peter 2:1-3)*
2. *Growing in Christ (vv. 4-8)*
3. *Growing as God's people (vv. 9-10)*

EXPLORING THE MEANING
1. Growing in the Lord (1 Peter 2:1-3)

Peter has already encouraged his readers to be holy and pure by obeying the truth of God's Word. Having done so, they can love one another in a pure heart (1 Peter 1:22). Now, as he continues, Peter challenges the people to lay aside malice, guile, hypocrisy, envy and every evil action.

Perhaps Peter recognized that these negative characteristics were a part of the society in which the suffering Christians lived. Certainly they could be contaminated by these things. Yet, Peter wants the people to live as "newborn babes" who need nourishment through the mother's milk. No baby can grow and live a healthy life without proper nourishment. We too must drink the "pure milk of the word" (v. 2) if we are to "taste" the glory of God and grow in knowledge and faith.

2. Growing in Christ (vv. 4-8)

Peter admonishes us to come to Jesus Christ who is the "living foundation of Rock upon which God builds" (v. 4, LB). Peter affirms that Jesus was rejected by men, but chosen by God to become a solid foundation for the church. Secondly, believers who put their trust in Christ are considered "living stones" who form a "building" where Jesus Christ can dwell. As a result, we can willingly give our time, gifts, and treasures to God.

Peter then uses three Old Testament passages to help support his belief that Christ is a living stone. First, the apostle quotes Isaiah 28:16 to show that Christ is the "chief cornerstone," who was chosen of God. Those who put their trust in Christ will not be ashamed in living a holy life or be frightened at His coming.

Secondly, Peter quotes Psalm 118:22 to show that Jesus Christ is precious to those who have accepted Him. Even though the Pharisees and religious leaders rejected Christ, the early Christians ultimately made Him the foundation of the house of God and the foundation of our salvation and eternal life.

Third, Peter quotes Isaiah 8:14. While Christ has become the means of salvation and eternal life to those who believe, He has become offensive to those who have rejected Him. Once again, the Pharisees and religious leaders of Jesus' day ultimately stumbled and fell because of their unbelief. Unbelievers today are still stumbling because of their disobedience to God's Word and refusing to accept the truth about Jesus. All who reject Jesus Christ will one day stumble into hell because of their disbelief.

3. Growing as God's people (vv. 9-10)

Peter encourages his readers by sharing they have been chosen by God, which means they are "a royal priesthood, a holy nation" and "[God's] own special people" (v. 9a, NKJV). In essence, Peter tells his readers they are special to God even as the nation Israel was special to Him. Because of Christ Jesus, we are a royal people, chosen by God and set apart so we might honor Him.

God has chosen us and set us apart to praise Him even in the midst of our sufferings and trials. We can affirm this truth and give God the praise when we recognize He has called us out of sin into His abiding presence.

The Prophet Isaiah tells us that "the people who walked in darkness have seen a great light. Those who dwelt in the land of the shadow of death, upon them a light has shined" (Isaiah 9:2, NKJV). God has brought us out of sin and death through the suffering of Jesus Christ, and brought us into the truth of His grace because of His great love for us.

Finally, Peter reminds the people that at one time they were not called by God and had no hope in Him. But now, as a result of God's love, we hold our heads high, knowing we have obtained the mercy of God because He lives in us. What a great blessing we have in Christ Jesus. His love and mercy have made us into people who are built solidly for Him. We are special—"a royal priesthood, a chosen race, and a holy nation" because God has called us that we might give praise to Him.

DISCERNING THE MEANING

1. *Why does Peter call the Scriptures the "pure milk of the word?"*
2. *What Old Testament Scriptures did Peter use to confirm Christ as chief cornerstone?*
3. *How were believers called out of sin and death?*
4. *Is it possible to obtain mercy from God without Christ? Why or why not?*

DECIDING MY RESPONSE

To think about—Some people have never heard of the mercy of God or experienced mercy from others. Why not help someone see that God's mercy is for the just and unjust alike? Often, the only hands, eyes and voice of God unbelievers hear and see are ours.

To do—This week commit to living and working as God's child. Sometimes that may be difficult, especially if one is working in a secular organization or living with those who are not saved. Allow your light to shine among unbelievers this week and watch God answer your prayers as you submit your will to His. Share what you learned with others next week.

WHAT I WILL DO

_____

_____

LIGHT ON THE HEAVY

Cornerstone—This is a term that has both a literal and figurative use in Scripture but is usually used figuratively (Psalm 118:22). Among the Canaanites, before the conquest of the land of Joshua, the laying of the foundation stone was accompanied by the dreadful rite of human sacrifice. Numerous skeletons have been unearthed, especially those of tiny babies in earthen jars.

Following rabbinical practice, which understood the term "cornerstone" in a Messianic context, the Synoptics validated the claim of Jesus of Nazareth to Messiahship by citation of Psalm 118:22. Also, we must understand the Pauline and Petrine usage of the word (quoting Isaiah 28:16 and 8:14, also Ephesians 2:20; 1 Peter 2:6) to get a clear meaning of its New Testament use. (*The Zondervan Pictorial Bible Dictionary,* 1967, p. 185)

Jesus Christ—Considerable help in understanding the personality and work of Christ may be gleaned from a consideration of the terms used to designate Him, especially as these are employed by Himself and His close associates. *Jesus* is used mostly in the narratives of the Gospels, and only rarely does it appear in direct address. It means Saviour, being related linguistically to the Hebrew name Joshua.

"Christ," meaning "anointed one," is the Greek equivalent to the Hebrew word "Messiah." Its function as a title is emphasized by the fact that often it occurs with the definite article, which gives it the force of "the promised Christ," the one who fulfills the concept of "Messiah" as set forth in the Old Testament Scriptures. (*The Zondervan Pictorial Bible Dictionary,* 1967, pp. 156-162).

Witnessing in the Midst of Suffering

DEFINING THE ISSUE

L loyd is a committed Christian who really loves the Lord. He has served faithfully in his church for the past seven years and heads the evangelism ministry.

Every Saturday Lloyd and his ministry partners are out on the streets of South Central Los Angeles, passing out tracts and sharing the Gospel with drug addicts, prostitutes and other street people. Through all his activities, Lloyd is suffering from lymphoma, a cancerous disease of the lymph nodes. Lloyd has gone to doctors and has undergone chemotherapy, but nothing can be done to arrest the disease.

Recently, someone asked Lloyd if he was bitter toward God because of his suffering. "Why no," he replied with a smile. "If our Lord can suffer, I guess I can, too."

Suffering is not new to believers in Christ. Some persons question whether we should suffer now that Christ has borne our sins on the cross. However, one of the most powerful witnesses to unbelievers is to see a child of God suffering and still maintaining his/her witness for Christ. Some may want to know how a person can suffer and still be joyful. What better way to lead a person to the Lord than by saying "The joy of God is in me and you can have the same joy if you desire."

In this study, the Apostle Peter continues his discussion to the "pilgrims of the Dispersion in Pontus, Galatia, Cappadocia, Asia, and Bithynia" (1 Peter 1:1, NKJV). By helping them see that suffering can be beneficial, he urges them to do good deeds.

AIM

By the end of the study participants should be able to:
1. *Explain the meaning of godly suffering.*
2. *Recognize some suffering has positive and spiritual benefits they may learn from.*
3. *Help someone who is suffering to know God cares about him/her.*

SCRIPTURE TEXT

1 PETER 3:13 And who is he that will harm you, if ye be followers of that which is good?

14 But and if ye suffer for righteousness' sake, happy are ye: and be not afraid of their terror, neither be troubled;

15 But sanctify the Lord God in your hearts: and be ready always to give an answer to every man that asketh you a reason of the hope that is in you with meekness and fear:

16 Having a good conscience; that, whereas they speak evil of you, as of evildoers, they may be ashamed that falsely accuse your good conversation in Christ.

17 For it is better, if the will of God be so, that ye suffer for well doing, than for evil doing.

18 For Christ also hath once suffered for sins, the just for the unjust, that he might bring us to God, being put to death in the flesh, but quickened by the Spirit:

1 PETER 4:1 Forasmuch then as Christ hath suffered for us in the flesh, arm yourselves likewise with the same mind: for he that hath suffered in the flesh hath ceased from sin;

2 That he no longer should live the rest of his time in the flesh to the lusts of men, but to the will of God.

7 But the end of all things is at hand: be ye therefore sober, and watch unto prayer.

8 And above all things have fervent charity among yourselves: for charity shall cover the multitude of sins.

9 Use hospitality one to another without grudging.

10 As every man hath received the gift, even so minister the same one to another, as good stewards of the manifold grace of God.

11 If any man speak, let him speak as the oracles of God; if any man minister, let him do it as of the ability which God giveth: that God in all things may be glorified through Jesus Christ, to whom be praise and dominion for ever and ever. Amen.

BIBLE BACKGROUND

The last lesson focused on how God has called us to be His people. Peter declared that we have been chosen by God to be a "royal priesthood" (1 Peter 2:9). We are a holy, special people who have been called out of sin and darkness into the marvelous light of God's love (1 Peter 2:9-10). As a result of God's calling, we should submit to earthly authorities, including the government (1 Peter 2:11-17), those who rule over us (vv. 18-25), and to one another in our homes (1 Peter 3:1-7). These teachings were extremely important to the early Christians who lived in a world that disagreed with the teachings of Christ.

Peter's desire was to see believers grow in the grace and knowledge of Christ Jesus despite the opposition they faced (see 2 Peter 3:18). Since the believers were under harsh rulership, it was important that Peter encourage them to live holy lives even in the face of suffering.

This lesson focuses on how a believer can be faithful despite suffering for our Lord. Let's see what Peter has to say about this important subject.

POINTS TO PONDER

1. *How can we be blessed?*
2. *Why should we sanctify our hearts?*
3. *What is the best way to suffer?*
4. *Why should we have the same mind of Christ?*
5. *How and why should we minister in the name of the Lord?*

THE LESSON AT-A-GLANCE

1. *The motivation for suffering (1 Peter 3:13-18)*
2. *The example of suffering (vv. 4:1-2)*
3. *The effects of godly suffering (vv. 7-11)*

EXPLORING THE MEANING

1. The motivation for suffering (1 Peter 3:13-18)

Peter encourages his listeners not to repay evil with evil or to be evil-minded. Why? Because Jesus Christ has promised blessings on those who walk in love and show compassion to others. Peter recognized that those who commit to living like Christ would suffer for their lifestyle and experience danger. But even if they should suffer for righteousness' sake, God would see them through. Therefore, they could stand without fear despite hardship and suffering.

Peter was not saying a person suffering for doing wrong would experience the blessings of God. On the contrary, those who have committed themselves to God and walk in His love would be able to stand in the midst of harsh treatment and suffering.

The apostle also exhorts the people to "sanctify the Lord God" in their hearts. Thus they would have an excellent testimony to share with anyone who wondered at their joy in spite of suffering. Secondly, Peter wanted the people to walk in meekness and reverence so their conscience would not be defamed and no one could accuse them of being evildoers. Christians are to walk in integrity and love so people can't accuse or mock them. Peter reminds us that our lifestyle is very important. How we behave toward others can make a difference.

Peter next shares one of the most important guidelines of the Christian faith. "It is the will of God [if we] suffer for doing good than for doing evil" (v. 17, NKJV). Some people may find this to be a strange principle. Why would God want us to suffer at all? His purpose is for us to live a godly and exemplary life so others can learn from our example. Yet, it is far better for us to suffer for doing good than for our sinful ways. God's name is defamed when His children fall into sin. Our motivation for suffering should be that Christ Jesus may be formed in us even while we are suffering.

To encourage us Peter gives us a good example of Christ, who suffered unjustly. Christ suffered and died for the sins of the world so He could redeem to the Father all who believe in Him, placing them into the body of Christ through His Spirit (v. 18). Christ's suffering was redemptive. Ours will be also.

2. The example of suffering (1 Peter 4:1-2)

Peter continues his discussion concerning Christ's suffering by sharing what believers are to do. We are to think as Christ did. If we take the same view of suffering as Christ did, we can break the dominion of sin in our lives and walk in the will of God, despite the afflictions we go through. Sometimes God uses suffering to mature us for His glory. While we may find pain to be an odd way to produce maturity in our lives, we need to ask God three questions when we suffer:

A. *What are You trying to teach me?*
B. *How can I glorify You?*
C. *With whom can I share my experience?*

3. The effects of godly suffering (vv. 7-11)

Peter now switches to another part of the subject of suffering. He believed that the imminent return of Jesus Christ was near. Therefore, he said Christians must be "of sound judgment and sober [in] spirit for the purpose of prayer" (v. 7, NASB). We can't allow ourselves to get entangled with the affairs of the world and pay evil for evil. Instead, the apostle encourages us to have a deep, fervent love for everyone because "love will cover a multitude of sins" (v. 8b, NKJV).

This does not mean that we become oblivious to sin or sweep it under the carpet. On the contrary, we must be patient with other people and lovingly forgive them when they transgress, even as Christ has forgiven us. Christian love must extend beyond the four walls of the church where we offer hospitality to all we meet. Once again, we must use Christ as our example. Since He gave freely, we must too.

We must also be willing to use our spiritual gifts to faithfully serve others. Since spiritual gifts come from God and are by His grace, we cannot withhold serving anyone, despite the suffering we may endure. By doing so, we show that we are "good stewards of the manifold grace of God" (v. 10, NKJV).

Finally, the apostle encourages Christians to speak and minister with a God-given ability so that Jesus Christ might be exalted in everything. He will thus have rule and honor over our lives even during our trials and sufferings.

Most normal people do not like to experience hardships and sufferings. However, if we are to emulate Christ, we can be assured that God will use our suffering as a powerful testimony to bring many to Him.

DISCERNING MY DUTY

1. What is the purpose of godly suffering?
2. Is it necessary for Christians to suffer? Why or why not?
3. How can we glorify God through our suffering?
4. What is the difference between godly and sinful suffering?

DECIDING MY RESPONSE

To think about—Many in our society are suffering from the effects of broken homes, joblessness and other economic woes. What can we do to alleviate suffering and show others how Christ can be seen in the core of brokenness?

To do—This week ask the Lord to show you the reason for suffering. Perhaps you may be going through some severe test. Ask God to help you learn from your suffering and how you might share your experience with another person who is also suffering. Report to the class next week.

WHAT I WILL DO

_____

_____

LIGHT ON THE HEAVY

Suffering—In the Bible suffering is regarded as an intrusion into this created world. All things were made good (Genesis 1:31). When sin entered, suffering also entered into the world in the form of conflict, pain, corruption, drudgery and death.

In bearing their witness to the suffering of the coming Messiah, the Old Testament writers were teaching how God can give a new meaning to suffering. Their own experience of serving God in Israel taught them that the love of God must involve sharing the affliction and shame as well as the slander of those they were seeking to redeem.

Suffering can have a new meaning for those who are members

of the body of Christ. They can share in the suffering of Christ, and regard themselves as committed to a career of suffering (1 Peter 4:1-2). (*The New Bible Dictionary,* 2nd ed., 1984, p. 1148)

Humble, Steadfast, Vigilant

DEFINING THE ISSUE

One of the most controversial aspects of Christianity is humility. Many of us think humble people suffer from low self-esteem. However, humble people are usually strong and full of self-control. They recognize that humility is the Christian way and don't mind being a servant to others. Secondly, most humble people know what the Bible says about Jesus who was the epitome of humility (see Philippians 2:5-9).

Another characteristic often overlooked is steadfastness. To be steadfast means to be determined and firmly fixed in one's place. Christians need not run and hide in the face of controversy or danger, but hold their ground against the devil and anything that hinders what God wants to do. Sometimes we confuse steadfastness with traditionalism. However, those who are truly steadfast know God's Word and recognize the importance of being stable and fixed in the middle of changing circumstances.

Vigilance is another attribute of the mature Christian. To be vigilant is to alertly watch for, and avoid danger. Those who are vigilant can see dangers from a distance and can notify others who can do something about them.

In this study we will explore these characteristics through the words of the Apostle Peter.

AIM

By the end of the study participants will:

1. Learn the characteristics of humility so they can be a blessing to someone in their home this week.

2. *Commit to being steadfast in the faith despite obstacles.*
3. *Discern the works of the devil so they can resist him this week.*

SCRIPTURE TEXT

1 PETER 5:1 The elders which are among you I exhort, who am also an elder, and a witness of the sufferings of Christ, and also a partaker of the glory that shall be revealed:

2 Feed the flock of God which is among you, taking the oversight thereof, not by constraint, but willingly; not for filthy lucre, but of a ready mind;

3 Neither as being lords over God's heritage, but being examples to the flock.

4 And when the chief Shepherd shall appear, ye shall receive a crown of glory that fadeth not away.

5 Likewise, ye younger, submit yourselves unto the elder. Yea, all of you be subject one to another, and be clothed with humility: for God resisteth the proud, and giveth grace to the humble.

6 Humble yourselves therefore under the mighty hand of God, that he may exalt you in due time:

7 Casting all your care upon him; for he careth for you.

8 Be sober, be vigilant; because your adversary the devil, as a roaring lion, walketh about, seeking whom he may devour:

9 Whom resist stedfast in the faith, knowing that the same afflictions are accomplished in your brethren that are in the world.

10 But the God of all grace, who hath called us unto his eternal glory by Christ Jesus, after that ye have suffered a while, make you perfect, stablish, strengthen, settle you.

11 To him be glory and dominion for ever and ever. Amen.

BIBLE BACKGROUND

The Apostle Peter continues his exhortation to the "strangers scattered" throughout the world. Peter warns that Christians will partake in the sufferings of Christ. We should not be surprised when we go through fiery trials. Instead we can rejoice, knowing that we are a part of Christ (see 1 Peter 4:12-14). Peter is quick to point out the difference between righteous and unrighteous suffering. Peter recognizes that there is no honor for those who suffer because they are busybodies, murderers, thieves or backbiters. These people cause much shame and reproach in the body of Christ and cannot glorify God through their suffering. After all, how can they commit their suffering to the Lord if their deeds are unrighteous?

Peter also makes it clear that one day judgment will begin at the house of God. All will stand before the Lord and be judged according to his/her deeds. That's why it is important for Christians to commit their ways to the Lord despite the sufferings they may endure. The apostle emphasizes that those who obey God's Word will be "scarcely saved" (1 Peter 4:18a). For those who disobey, their end will be ultimate destruction.

Peter concludes his opening epistle by giving encouragement to the elders and young Christians so they might be vigilant in their faith.

POINTS TO PONDER

1. Whom did Peter exhort?

2. What did he want them to do?

3. What will they receive when Christ appears?

4. Why should believers humble themselves?

5. How should believers conduct themselves?

6. Why does God permit suffering in our lives?

THE LESSON AT-A-GLANCE

1. A call for humility (1 Peter 5:1-4)

2. A call for submission (vv. 5-7)

3. A call for vigilance (vv. 8-11)

EXPLORING THE MEANING
1. A call for humility (1 Peter 5:1-4)

Peter's charge to the elders of the church is based on his own experience as an elder. In this epistle, he knows the responsibilities involved with being an elder and he wants those who are in charge of the church to be good examples.

Peter reminds his readers that he is "a fellow elder and a witness of the sufferings of Christ" (v. 1a). Peter was there when Christ suffered for the sins of the world. He was given the charge to feed Christ's sheep before our Lord's ascension (see John 21:15-21). Peter was also the first spokesman for the Christian church; he saw it grow. Therefore, he was aware of the glory that would be revealed to the church through Christ.

Christ had called Peter to be a shepherd. Peter knew what it meant to feed, care for, guide and protect God's "little ones." Peter did not want the elders to be forced to shepherd the flock. Instead, his desire was to see Christian leaders do so with an honest heart and not for financial gain. These men should be as overseers, ones who spiritually and physically guard the "sheep" against any harmful thing. Peter wanted these Christians to shepherd the flock "eagerly."

Such a person must have a shepherd's heart and be willing to put in long hours, showing consistent but thoughtful leadership, and longing to see God's people grow. The person who goes into ministry for the money is likely to be disappointed. There are thousands of jobs that pay more money. To enjoy the ministry, one must be called by God and be willing to give unselfishly of him/herself.

Peter didn't want these elders to "lord" over the people or rule with an iron fist. Instead, the apostle encouraged them to be examples to the flock. God does not want anyone to "lord" over His people. Pastors and other ministers are to be servants, freely giving to those in the congregation and living an exemplary life so that others might follow them as they follow Christ.

What is the reward for people who follow the apostle's words and serve God's people? One day Christ, who is the "Chief Shepherd," will return and give a "crown of glory" to those who have served faithfully, not looking for earthly rewards. That is why we must not serve the Lord only for money. As we give of ourselves in service to Him, we store up treasures in our "heavenly bank account." The riches we receive will never fade away and we can be assured that God has not forgotten one act of service performed in His name. Unlike those who may try to short-change us for the work we do, God will always be faithful and reward us no matter how small the job may be.

2. A call for submission (vv. 5-7)

Peter also addresses the "young people" (v. 5, NKJV) in the church. This doesn't necessarily mean the children. Instead, these are the sheep who are led by the church elders. If elders are to lead properly, they must have cooperative "sheep" who will submit themselves with reverence to the Lord. While it is important that elders lovingly guide the people, it is also important for the people to follow godly leadership so they can be instructed in the godly principles.

Secondly, Peter encourages elders and "sheep," both old and young, to submit to one another by "clothing" themselves with humility. In essence, Peter admonishes believers to live a humble and submissive life so they might imitate Jesus Christ who is the perfect model of humility (John 13:3-14).

Why should one live a humble life? Because "God resists the proud, but [He] gives grace to the humble" (v. 5b, NKJV). Selfish pride is a disgrace before God. We have nothing to be proud about since God has given us His righteousness, salvation, sanctification and redemption. Therefore, when we "puff up" ourselves, God has a way of bringing us down. Consequently, as we humble ourselves God will give us grace and exalt us in His own time (v. 6). The Scriptures tell us that "no one from the east or the west or from the desert can exalt a man. But it is God who judges: He brings one down, He exalts another" (Psalm 75:6, NIV).

Once we humble ourselves we can cast all our cares on the Lord because of His great love and concern for us (v. 7). The word "cast" denotes throwing a line into the water to catch fish. What Peter means is to throw everything that disturbs us onto our heavenly Father who is concerned about everything that concerns us. God loves each of His children in a special way. Therefore, He will comfort us so that our sorrows and woes can be easily borne.

3. A call for vigilance (vv. 8-11)

Peter recognized that believers must put their faith in God in order to walk soberly and vigilantly before Him. The New International Version (NIV) illuminates verse eight very profoundly. Believers must be full of self-control and alert at all times. Why? Because the devil, our enemy and adversary, is always looking for opportunities to viciously devour God's people through lies, deceits, sickness, bitterness and other negative characteristics. Peter compares Satan's attacks to those of a "roaring lion." Believers in Peter's time could relate to this since Nero would throw Christians in the Roman Coliseum to be mauled to death by the lions.

The devil must be resisted (see James 4:7) and believers must be steadfast in the faith. We can only do so if we put our trust in Christ. However, we are not alone in our sufferings. We can find comfort in knowing that there are believers who are suffering for their faith around the world. We can be assured that if they can stand firm in the midst of suffering, we can too.

Peter also encouraged believers to endure suffering. It would mature their faith, establish them in the things of God, strengthen and settle believers in Christ. That way, they won't be tossed "to and fro" with every new doctrine that comes their way (see Ephesians 4:14). God's grace will be the helping power to bring this about, and one day we will experience the glory of the Lord in the fullest.

The apostle concludes this portion of the letter with a benediction for the church. "To Jesus Christ belongs all the glory and the dominion forever and ever. Amen" (v. 11, NKJV). Only Jesus can help us be humble in our walk with Christ, steadfast in our faith, and vigilant in our fight against the devil.

DISCERNING MY DUTY

1. *Why is it important that we cast our care on the Lord? How can we do that?*
2. *How can we resist the devil? Discuss.*
3. *What is the crown of glory? How will believers receive it?*
4. *How can believers be exalted in a world of pride and rebellion?*

DECIDING MY RESPONSE

To think about—Suffering is a part of perfecting and maturing people for kingdom work. How can you help those who are suffering to understand that they can turn their miseries and woes into learning experiences? Be willing to share this truth: People must first change their attitudes toward their circumstances. Their "attitude will determine their altitude." Be prepared to share your experiences with your classmates next week.

To do—This week spend time cultivating the qualities of humility, steadfastness and vigilance by: (1) serving others; (2) being committed to a project despite obstacles; and (3) resisting the devil by overcoming temptations that may come your way this week. Be prepared to give a report to the class next week.

WHAT I WILL DO

LIGHT ON THE HEAVY

Devil—This is one of the principal titles of Satan, the arch-enemy of God and of humankind. Thirty-five times in the New Testament the word refers to Satan; but in the King James Version the same word is used about 60 times to render the Greek *daimonion* which is properly translated "demon" in the Authorized Standard Version. Apparently, God initially created a hierarchy of holy angels, of whom one of the highest orders was the cherubim. One of them, perhaps the highest of all, was "the anointed cherub that covereth" (Ezekiel 28:14), who was created beautiful and perfect in his ways. This cherub knew he was beautiful, but pride entered his heart and the first recorded sin in the whole history of eternity occurred. Pride led to self-will (Isaiah 14:13-14) and self-will to rebellion. This great cherub became "Satan" the adversary of God, and apparently led other angels into rebellion.

God then created man in His own image. Because Satan already hated God, he hated man and tried to destroy him. It is evident that God could have destroyed Satan at the moment he became "Satan," but God has tolerated him these many millenia. He has used him over the ages for testing people. In the age-long conflict between good and evil, it sometimes seems as though God has given Satan every advantage. Even so, God's victory is certain. *(The Zondervan Pictorial Bible Dictionary, 1967, pp. 215-216)*

Growing in Grace

DEFINING THE ISSUE

Mrs. Temperton didn't know what to expect when she had her first baby. She was 47 years old and a senior vice president at the telephone company. With patience, determination, hard work and prayer, Mrs. Temperton lovingly raised her child.

She always thanked God for her baby and made sure she or her husband spent adequate time with him. In this way the baby's self-esteem wouldn't be damaged. She often read Bible verses and sang praise songs to the child so the baby would grow spiritually as well as physically. Though Mrs. Temperton wasn't a "seasoned" mother, she was determined to provide her child with everything necessary to ensure he would mature in every area of life.

Often we are more concerned about physical growth than spiritual growth. Yet it is important that we grow in every area of life. It is especially important that we grow spiritually. As we grow in God's wisdom, knowledge and understanding, we can impart what we learn to others. Certainly, all of us need to experience God's power and anointing in our lives so we can impart the same to others. By increasing our knowledge of the Word of God, we can give to others what God has given to us.

In this study the Apostle Peter will help us understand the importance of growing in the grace of God. Once we receive understanding on how the grace of God is vital for us, we can impart the same knowledge to others.

AIM

By the end of the study participants should be able to:

1. *Discover whether the fruit of the Spirit has been developed in their lives.*

2. *Commit to growing in the grace and knowledge of Jesus Christ this week by establishing a consistent study pattern.*

3. *Help someone else grow in grace by sharing the principles of the lesson and spending quality time with that person.*

SCRIPTURE TEXT

2 PETER 1:1 Simon Peter, a servant and an apostle of Jesus Christ, to them that have obtained like precious faith with us through the righteousness of God and our Saviour Jesus Christ:

2 Grace and peace be multiplied unto you through the knowledge of God, and of Jesus our Lord,

3 According as his divine power hath given unto us all things that pertain unto life and godliness, through the knowledge of him that hath called us to glory and virtue:

4 Whereby are given unto us exceeding great and precious promises: that by these ye might be partakers of the divine nature, having escaped the corruption that is in the world through lust.

5 And beside this, giving all diligence, add to your faith virtue; and to virtue knowledge;

6 And to knowledge temperance; and to temperance patience; and to patience godliness;

7 And to godliness brotherly kindness; and to brotherly kindness charity.

8 For if these things be in you, and abound, they make you that ye shall neither be barren nor unfruitful in the knowledge of our Lord Jesus Christ.

9 But he that lacketh these things is blind, and cannot see afar off, and hath forgotten that he was purged from his old sins.

10 Wherefore the rather, brethren, give diligence to make your calling and election sure: for if ye do these things, ye shall never fall:

11 For so an entrance shall be ministered unto you abundantly into the everlasting kingdom of our Lord and Saviour Jesus Christ.

12 Wherefore I will not be negligent to put you always in

remembrance of these things, though ye know them, and be established in the present truth.

13 Yea, I think it meet, as long as I am in this tabernacle, to stir you up by putting you in remembrance;

14 Knowing that shortly I must put off this my tabernacle, even as our Lord Jesus Christ hath shewed me.

BIBLE BACKGROUND

Dallas Theological Seminary professor Kenneth Gangel suggests that Second Peter could be entitled "the believer's conflict in the latter days" *(Epistle to Second Peter,* The Bible Knowledge Commentary, 1982, pp. 859-879). The Apostle Peter's focus was on how believers could live despite the problems of the last days. Peter emphasized that believers should live a holy and godly life even as they looked forward to the day when Christ would return.

In writing Second Peter, the apostle addressed his letter to both Jews and Gentiles (1 Peter 1:1). Peter was a concerned pastor who desired to see Christian people mature. Peter recognized his time was short, so his challenge was to help believers mature in the faith of Christ despite the false teachings making headway in the community. Peter also gave his readers hope by sharing with them the assurance that Jesus Christ would return.

As we begin this study Peter is challenging his readers to be diligent in their faith through the knowledge of Jesus Christ.

POINTS TO PONDER

1. *To whom was Peter writing his letter?*
2. *How are grace and peace given to believers?*
3. *What have believers received through God's divine power?*
4. *What should we add to our faith through diligence?*
5. *How can we be fruitful in the knowledge of Jesus Christ?*
6. *How can we keep from stumbling?*

THE LESSON AT-A-GLANCE

1. *The promise of sharing Christ's nature (2 Peter 1:1-4)*
2. *The challenge of Christian growth (vv. 5-11)*
3. *The power of a Christian life (vv. 12-14)*

EXPLORING THE MEANING
1. The promise of sharing Christ's nature (2 Peter 1:1-4)

Peter begins his salutation by identifying himself as a "servant and apostle of Jesus Christ" (v. 1a). Peter recognized the reality of walking in Jesus' footsteps as a servant (see John 21:15-17, 22). His desire was to follow Jesus not only as a servant but also as an apostle, which means "one who is sent."

Peter addressed his letter to those "who have obtained like precious faith" (v. 1b) just as he had. However, Peter recognized that our faith has been obtained through the righteousness of God which is based on our Lord and Saviour Jesus Christ. Only through Jesus have we received the divine nature of God. That is why Isaiah tells us that "all our righteousness are like filthy rags" (Isaiah 64:6b, NKJV). No matter how moral, upright or pious we may be, the only way we can come to God is through the merits of the death and resurrection of Jesus Christ.

The apostle abundantly extends "grace and peace" upon the people. Yet his blessing and desire are that they come into the full knowledge of God and Christ. Thus, they would have the tools needed to destroy the false teachings invading the church. Peter also wanted the people to understand that God had given each believer His divine power to ensure a victorious spiritual life. Once again, we can obtain God's divine power for victorious living through an intimate knowledge of our Saviour. In essence, Jesus has called many to Himself by His divine nature and power, available to everyone who trusts Him.

Jesus Christ has also given believers "exceedingly great and precious promises" of eternal life and supernatural power for holy living. This will be accomplished by the Holy Spirit's dwelling within us. As we share in the very life of God, we have the authority and power to overcome, or escape, the corruption and depravity that is in the world. In essence, God gives us overcoming power so that we can defeat the power of the enemy. Then nothing shall be able to hurt us (see Luke 11:17-19).

2. The challenge of divine growth (vv. 5-11)

Peter challenges his readers to grow spiritually in order to experience the benefits of God's divine nature within. He gives us practical examples on what we should do. First, we must be persistent in our faith and walk with God by giving careful attention to what we do and say. That way, we can be earnest in our effort to live in a godly manner.

Secondly, Peter says that we must add virtue to our faith. Virtue means to conform to a standard of righteousness that has been established by God. While we aren't righteous in ourselves, we must live in a way that makes moral uprightness, an integral part of our lives. Once we establish moral uprightness, we can operate with godly knowledge, self-control, patience, perseverance, godliness, brotherly kindness and *agape* love. (vv. 5-8). The characteristics outlined by Peter are the fruit of the Holy Spirit (Galatians 5:22-23). There is no way we can embody the fruit of the Spirit until we have the Holy Spirit within us. Godly knowledge can help us live self-controlled lives. Self-control can help us persevere under the pressures of life. Perseverance helps shape our character in a godly way. Godliness is the key to agape love that enables us to love our brothers and sisters as Christ commands.

The apostle affirms that if these characteristics are formed in us, we will be spirit-led Christians who are full of the knowledge of Jesus Christ. On the other hand, if we lack spiritual fruit Peter says we are "shortsighted, even to blindness" (v. 9) because we have lost sight of what God has done for us.

Therefore, we must be confident and diligent to make sure our faith, virtue and knowledge are based on the rock of Jesus Christ. In this way what we profess won't be based on heresy or someone else's testimony. Instead, our own godly calling will be sure as we bear spiritual fruit in our lives. The spiritual fruit of righteousness will help us live an abundant life here on earth. We will then establish an "entrance. . . . into the everlasting kingdom of our Lord and Saviour Jesus Christ" by the way we live (v. 11).

3. The power of a Christian life (vv. 12-14)

The apostle affirms that it is his duty to remind the early church of the importance of developing their faith through godly living. Even though we may know these things and are presently established in Bible truths, it is good to be reminded daily of God's Word.

The Scriptures tell us that faith comes by hearing the Word of God (Romans 10:17). That is why it is important that we come to church and hear sermons that can help us to mature in Christ. Some people may not realize how important it is to attend a church where the Bible is honored and taught. If we are going to grow and live a surrendered life for the Lord, we must hear the Word. Its truths must be reinforced in us as often as possible.

Peter states that as long as he is "in this tent" (v. 13), in his human body, he will remind believers of the truth and do all he can to establish the truth in their lives. Once the gifts are stirred up in us, we can live victorious and godly lives in the midst of corruption and sin.

Finally, Peter tells them that he must soon take off his tent—or die—just as Jesus did. Yet, Peter's job, like ours, is to remind others of the importance of living like Jesus Christ who is the author and perfecter of our faith (Hebrews 12:2).

DISCERNING MY DUTY

1. *How important is diligence in the Christian faith? Discuss.*
2. *What are the precious promises that God has given His children?*
3. *Why is it important that we be continually reminded of God's truth?*
4. *How do we grow in grace? Discuss.*

DECIDING MY RESPONSE

To think about—Everyone should desire to grow holistically, but some people have lost their desire to grow. What principles can you take from today's lesson to help motivate someone to return to school or take on a new hobby? Be creative in your thinking.

To do—This week examine your own life to see whether the fruit of the Spirit is being established in your life. What must you take off or put on to develop godly fruit? Write out a plan of action to be followed up on throughout the week. Report your activities to the class next week.

WHAT I WILL DO

_____

_____

LIGHT ON THE HEAVY

Election—Since the whole of humanity is fallen into sinful living from which it cannot rescue itself, none will be saved without the redeeming grace of God. The sovereign choice of God, as to who may receive this grace, is based on election.

Election is God's eternal and fixed rule to exclude corrupt people who, because of their sin, deserve death. He provides the source of salvation through Christ to those He will save. He will achieve this through the work of the Holy Spirit.

Biblical usage of the word "election" centers primarily in *eklektos*, a Greek adjective signifying "the chosen," and in *ekloge*, as a noun, signifying "that which is chosen." *Ekloge* is used almost invariably in the New Testament to refer to individuals. In its more restricted sense, it refers to the election of people to salvation.

The source of election is in God alone. The cause of election is at least twofold: God's compassionate mercy extended toward people in Christ (without which no person would be saved), and His own glory. Election assures that the redemptive grace of God will draw sick and evil hearts into loving fellowship and responsive obedience to God. Armenians insist that election is conditional, contingent on the proper acceptance of God's grace available to all. *(The Zondervan Bible Pictorial Dictionary, 1967, p. 242)*

Asia—A Roman province which in the first three centuries A.D. included nearly the whole of the western part of Asia Minor and some of the coastal islands such as Samos and Patmos. By the end of the first century A.D., Christianity was strongly represented in the provincial cities, and was the enmity of Jewish and Greek populations.

The epistles of Peter are addressed to the Dispersion in Pontus, Galatia, Cappadocia, Asia, and Bithynia. These names are all to be taken in their provincial sense. Bithynia, though forbidden to Paul, must have received the Gospel early. The Roman governor Pliny found Christianity in great strength in Pontus (rather than Bithynia proper). Hort argued that the list in First Peter represents the sequence of Silvanus' projected route. This was probably done using the important road from Amisus on the Pontic coast through Amasia in Pontus Galaticus, in the eastern part of what was then the province of Galatia. Second Peter is thought to be addressed to the same recipients of Asia Minor (see 2 Peter 3:1). *(The International Standard Bible Encyclopedia,* Vol. 1, 1979, Grand Rapids, Michigan: William B. Eerdmans Publishing Co., pp. 322-328).

Focused On The Future

DEFINING THE ISSUE

Have you ever thought about the future and what's in store for the world? Certainly the Scriptures help us understand God's eternal plan. But what about us? What will happen to our children, our way of life, and society as a whole? How will our environment hold up against the ravages of pollution, diseases and other problems that plague us daily?

In our Bible text the Apostle Peter urges us to focus on the future and to the time when Jesus Christ will return. Peter reminds his readers of the new heavens and earth that will appear when the Righteous Judge comes to reign forever. Let's see what the apostle has to say about this timely truth.

AIM

By the end of the study participants should be able to:

1. *Describe the events which the Apostle Peter says will precede the arrival of the new heavens and new earth.*
2. *Commit to sharing the Gospel with an unsaved relative or friend.*
3. *Review 2 Peter and clarify reasons why God desires everyone to be saved.*

SCRIPTURE TEXT

2 PETER 3:3 Knowing this first, that there shall come in the last days scoffers, walking after their own lusts,

4 And saying, Where is the promise of his coming? for since the fathers fell asleep, all things continue as they were from the

beginning of the creation.

5 For this they willingly are ignorant of, that by the word of God the heavens were of old, and the earth standing out of the water and in the water:

6 Whereby the world that then was, being overflowed with water, perished:

7 But the heavens and the earth, which are now, by the same word are kept in store, reserved unto fire against the day of judgment and perdition of ungodly men.

8 But, beloved, be not ignorant of this one thing, that one day is with the Lord as a thousand years, and a thousand years as one day.

9 The Lord is not slack concerning his promise, as some men count slackness; but is longsuffering to us-ward, not willing that any should perish, but that all should come to repentance.

10 But the day of the Lord will come as a thief in the night; in the which the heavens shall pass away with a great noise, and the elements shall melt with fervent heat, the earth also and the works that are therein shall be burned up.

11 Seeing then that all these things shall be dissolved, what manner of persons ought ye to be in all holy conversation and godliness,

12 Looking for and hasting unto the coming of the day of God, wherein the heavens being on fire shall be dissolved, and the elements shall melt with fervent heat?

13 Nevertheless we, according to his promise, look for new heavens and a new earth, wherein dwelleth righteousness.

14 Wherefore, beloved, seeing that ye look for such things, be diligent that ye may be found of him in peace, without spot, and blameless.

BIBLE BACKGROUND

In the previous lesson the Apostle Peter encouraged the church to grow in the faith and knowledge of Jesus Christ who is our example of faith and life. Peter expounds on the characteristics believers must have which include virtue, self-control, godliness and love. Secondly, Peter admonishes us to be diligent in our faith so that we are sure of our salvation and can articulate the truth to others.

Peter also denounces the false teachers that were making inroads into the church during his day. That's why he makes one of the most profound statements of the New Testament: "No prophecy of Scripture is of any private interpretation, for prophecy never came by the will of man, but holy men of God spoke as they were moved by the Holy Spirit" (2 Peter 1:20-21, NKJV). Peter hammers his point home by calling the false teachers "spots and blemishes . . . accursed children" (2 Peter 2:13-14, NKJV). He also predicts that they will be destroyed by the lust and heresy they have spread throughout the community of faith. Now, as we begin today's lesson, Peter reminds his readers of the truth of the future, that Jesus Christ will return soon.

POINTS TO PONDER

1. *What will happen in the last days?*
2. *According to Peter, how was the world created?*
3. *For what is the world reserved?*
4. *How does the Lord "count" time?*
5. *How will we know when the Lord returns?*
6. *How should believers conduct themselves until the Lord returns?*

THE LESSON AT-A-GLANCE

1. *The Lord's promises are sure (2 Peter 3:3-7)*
2. *The Lord's judgment is sure (vv. 8-9)*
3. *The Lord's return is sure (vv. 10-14)*

EXPLORING THE MEANING
1. The Lord's promises are sure (2 Peter 3:3-7)

Peter shares a sobering fact with the church. Despite the truth of the Gospel and the reality that Jesus Christ will return one day, the apostle tells us that "scoffers will come in the last days" mocking the truth. These are people who do their own thing, live according to their own truth, and reject anything related to the Gospel. As a matter of fact these people have the same attitude as those in Noah's day. God affirmed that He would destroy the earth because of its wickedness and instructed Noah to build an ark. Once Noah got inside the ark, God destroyed the earth with a great flood (see Genesis 6 8).

Despite God's judgment against the world, the people have forgotten what took place simply because "all things continue as they were from the beginning of creation" (2 Peter 3:4, NKJV). In essence, the sun continues to rise and shine, human beings continue to breathe, nature continues to bloom and we seem to have an abundance of water. So, what has changed since the foundation of the world? How do we know that Jesus is to return? Certainly, scoffers and unbelievers can point to the stability of the world and say, "How can you say that Jesus is to return when everything is the same?" Yet, in spite of all arguments to the contrary, we believe Jesus will return as He promised.

Peter also states that scoffers "willfully forget" the truth. They know that God "spoke" the heavens, earth, and its elements into existence from nothing, and that the same world also perished by the flood. Therefore, they are without excuse and will one day perish because of their willful ignorance. However, the world in which we live is kept together by the same word that God spoke in the beginning. One day God will judge the world with fire and purge the earth of ungodly men so that His kingdom can be established.

2. The Lord's judgment is sure (vv. 8-9)

Peter now turns his attention to believers. In case they should question why the Lord is "slow" in returning to judge the world, Peter helps believers understand His motivation and purposes. To the Lord, one day is as a thousand years and a thousand years is as one day. God's timetable is different from ours. The psalmist tells us that "a thousand years in [God's] sight are like yesterday when it is past, and like a watch in the night" (Psalm 90:4, NKJV). One writer observes that earthlings see time against time; but God sees time against eternity. In fact, time only seems long because of our finite perspective.

Why is this an important truth? The Lord is patient with human beings. His desire is for every person to come to repentance and be saved. Therefore, God is not slow concerning His promises toward us. He is long-suffering or patient toward sinners and His promises are sure toward His children. God is not interested in people going to hell and burning. But the reality is that not everyone will be saved. Yet, God is patiently waiting, wanting to see everyone come to the knowledge of the truth. The Scriptures tell us that God will not cast away anyone who, by faith, comes to Him (see John 6:37).

3. The Lord's return is sure (vv. 10-14)

Peter describes what will happen when the Lord returns. Peter calls it "the day of the Lord" (v. 10a, NKJV) and says it will take place suddenly and unexpectantly, like "a thief in the night." A thief doesn't announce when he is breaking into a house. Thieves are usually unpredictable. So it is with the Lord's return. No one knows the day or hour when Jesus will return. But when the "Day of the Lord" occurs, "the heavens will pass away with a great noise" and the stars, moon and other elements in the universe will be destroyed and melted by fire. Not only will the world be shaken, but every person's works will be exposed, or "laid bare." In essence, no one will be able to escape the fury and wrath of the Lord.

The apostle raises an important point that may have been on the minds of many people. Peter says that since the world will be melted, and every person's works will be laid bare, "what manner of persons ought you to be in holy conduct and godliness"? (v. 11, NKJV) We need to ask this question of ourselves today. Our lives must reflect godliness and holiness at all times. We don't know who is watching us and reading our lives. That's why it is imperative that we walk in holiness so that our lives reflect the Lord Jesus Christ. As we live godly and holy lives, we can look forward to the day when the Lord returns.

Once the old world has melted away, we can look for new heavens and a new earth. Righteousness and holiness will dwell there. We live in a world where rebellion and ungodliness are prevalent. However, we can still rejoice today because we know the promises of God are as sure as His Word. Because God has promised us a home where righteousness and peace will abound, we should be motivated to do all we can to spread this good news to everyone we know.

Finally, Peter admonishes the church to be diligent and determined to live holy and blameless until the day of the Lord's return. Also, the apostle challenges his readers to live in peace. While our world may be in turmoil, Christians can dwell in peace and love because of our abiding relationship with Jesus Christ.

Certainly Peter's words can help us see a brighter day despite what we may go through. One day Jesus Christ will return to take us to be with Him. This is a wonderful future to look forward to.

DISCERNING MY DUTY

1. What does Peter mean when he says the world is reserved for fire?
2. Why is a thousand years like a day and a day like a thousand years to the Lord?
3. Does Peter teach universal salvation? Why or why not?
4. Is Peter suggesting that the world will melt and decay? If so, what will happen to its inhabitants? Discuss.
5. What would believers do who seriously believe what Peter teaches in this text?

DECIDING MY RESPONSE

To think about—Peter affirms that people have scoffed at the idea of the Lord's return for years. What tangible proof can you point an unbeliever to, to affirm that God is real and that one day He will return? Discuss.

To do—This week spend time meditating on the future and what it will be like when the Lord returns. Since Peter gives us an idea of what will happen to the world, spend time praying for unbelieving relatives and others who scoff at the idea that Jesus will return. Write their names in a prayer journal and ask the Lord to open their eyes to the truth before it's too late.

WHAT I WILL DO

_____

_____

LIGHT ON THE HEAVY

Heaven—Several words are translated "heaven," but the most important ones are the Hebrew *samayim* and the Greek *ouranos*. The former is plural, and the latter often occurs in the plural. But, just as with English, there does not seem to be any great difference between "heaven" and "the heavens." The term is used to describe the physical heaven. Heaven is the abode of God and of those closely associated with Him. The ancient Israelites were instructed to pray, "Look down from thy holy habitation, from heaven." God is the God of heaven, or the Lord. Among many ancient peoples there was the thought of the multiplicity of heavens. It has been suggested that the New Testament bears witness to the rabbinic idea of seven heavens, for there are references to Paradise (Luke 23:43), and to the third heaven. Jesus is also said to have passed through the heavens (Hebrews 4:14). There is also an eschatological use of the term. In both the Old and New Testaments, it is recognized that the present physical universe is not eternal, but will vanish and be replaced by "new heavens and a new earth" (Isaiah 65:17; 66:22; 2 Peter 3:10-13; Revelation 21:1). *(The New Bible Dictionary,* 2nd ed., 1984, pp. 465-466)

Keep On Loving

DEFINING THE ISSUE

Love is one of the virtues the Apostle Paul mentions in his letter to the Corinthians (see 1Corinthians 13). According to Paul love is supreme over any gifts we may have, whether it be prophecy, knowledge, or even faith.

Paul explains in his letter to the Corinthians is that agape love is patient, kind, not easily provoked, bears all things, endures all things, and will never fail. Now someone may ask, "How do I acquire that kind of love so that those characteristics are part of my life?" It is not easy—apart from divine empowerment. Often we face unbearable situations, in which our patience is tested to the limit, or where we cannot endure any more in our own strength.

However, when we allow the love of Jesus Christ to permeate our life, we can be patient and endure no matter what is going on around us. God desires that we not only love others, but that we abide in *His* love continuously. As we do, we discover how to love others and give of ourselves even when we don't feel like it.

There is something about "abiding" that makes the difference. When we abide, we are more consistent in our actions, regardless of the circumstances. And, when we abide in God's love, we seek the highest good of others because God does the same with us.

In this study we will investigate what it means to abide in God's love. As members of His family we have no room for hatred, deception, or sin. Instead, as we walk in the love and light of Jesus Christ, He becomes perfected in our lives and others will be able to see we belong to Him.

AIM

By the end of the study participants will:

1. *Have examined their lives to see how their motive for love compares with John's admonition in today's lesson.*

2. *Become convinced that remaining in God's love is the best option for the believer, and will determine to change their thoughts and actions toward God and others.*

SCRIPTURE TEXT

1 JOHN 1:1 That which was from the beginning, which we have heard, which we have seen with our eyes, which we have looked upon, and our hands have handled, of the Word of life;

2 (For the life was manifested, and we have seen it, and bear witness, and show unto you that eternal life, which was with the Father, and was manifested unto us;)

3 That which we have seen and heard declare we unto you, that ye also may have fellowship with us: and truly our fellowship is with the Father, and with His Son Jesus Christ.

4 And these things write we unto you, that your joy may be full.

5 This then is the message which we have heard of him, and declare unto you, that God is light, and in him is no darkness at all.

6 If we say that we have fellowship with him, and walk in darkness, we lie, and do not the truth:

7 But if we walk in the light, as he is in the light, we have fellowship with one another, and the blood of Jesus Christ his Son cleanseth us from all sin.

8 If we say that we have no sin, we deceive ourselves, and the truth is not in us.

9 If we confess our sins, he is faithful and just to forgive us our sins, and to cleanse us from all unrighteousness.

10 If we say that we have not sinned, we make him a liar, and his word is not in us.

1 JOHN 2:1 My little children, these things write I unto you, that ye sin not. And if any man sin, we have an advocate with the Father, Jesus Christ the righteous:

2 And he is the propitiation for our sins: and not for ours only, but also for the sins of the whole world.

3 And hereby we do know that we know him, if we keep his commandments.

4 He that saith, I know him, and keepeth not His commandments, is a liar, and the truth is not in him.

5 But whoso keepeth his word, in him verily is the love of God perfected: hereby know we that we are in him.
6 He that saith he abideth in him ought himself also so to walk, even as he walked.

BIBLE BACKGROUND

The Epistles of John are practical letters addressed to Christian readers. The First Epistle warns against the dangers of false teaching and challenges believers to obey God and love one another. One of the main themes in the epistle is fellowship with God the Father and the Son, Jesus Christ.

Bible scholars generally agree that the Epistles of John were written by John the Apostle, the son of Zebedee. Although his name does not appear in his letter, its tone suggests John's spiritual maturity and insight of the incarnate life of Jesus Christ.

Strong tradition says that John spent his old age in Ephesus. Since the letter doesn't give a specific place of origin, it has been thought that John wrote this and the other Epistles after he wrote the Gospel and before the persecution under Domitian in 95. That would probably place its writing in the late 80s or early 90s *Ryrie Study Bible*, 1982, p. 1912).

John's main purpose for writing is to refute Gnosticism the false teaching that had arisen in the churches during his day. Many have thought that Gnosticism had a great influence on the people. Among its teachings: (1) knowledge is superior to virtue; (2) the non-literal sense of Scripture is correct and can be understood only by a select few; (3) evil in the world precludes God being the only Creator; (4) the incarnation is incredible because deity cannot unite itself with anything material such as a body; and (5) there is no resurrection of the flesh. The ethical standards of many Gnostics were low, so John emphasized the reality of the incarnation and the high ethical standard of the earthly life of Christ (Ryrie, cited above.) As we begin our lesson, John is addressing the church, letting them know the importance of Jesus Christ and how His life benefits them.

POINTS TO PONDER

1. *To whom is John referring when he speaks of the Word of life?*

2. Why do you think John emphasized that he had "seen," "heard," and "handled," the Word of life?
3. If we walk in darkness and claim we have fellowship with God, what does that make us?
4. Who is the believer's advocate?
5. How can we "know" God?

THE LESSON AT-A-GLANCE

1. John's purpose for writing (1 John 1:1-4)
2. John's message of fellowship (vv. 5—2:2)
    A.   God is light (vv. 5-6)
    B.   God forgives (vv. 7-10)
    C.   God cleanses (2:1-2)
3. John's exhortation of abiding (vv. 3-6)

EXPLORING THE MEANING
1. John's purpose for writing (1 John 1:1-4)

John begins the first epistle, just as he did with the Gospel, with a prologue. The purpose of his prologue was to affirm the reality of Christ's incarnation and to affirm his audience's joy as they believe in this reality. Therefore, the apostle writes about the things which relate to Jesus Christ ("That which was from the beginning").

The life of Jesus Christ was manifested, or revealed, not only to the apostles, but also to others, who didn't know or receive Him (see John 1:10-11). But John had seen the historical Jesus and had given witness and testimony to others that eternal life, which was given by the Father, was actually manifested in the Son. This manifestation was also given to the apostles during the earthly ministry of Jesus.

John moves to his basic point of the prologue: that he might share the message of eternal life, which is found in Jesus Christ, with those to whom he was writing. Why? That they may have fellowship with him and other Christians who are in fellowship with the Father and the Son. Finally, John concludes the prologue by telling the church that his reason for writing to them was so their "joy may be full" (v. 4).

2. John's message of fellowship (vv. 5 2:2)
A. God is light (vv. 5-6).

John is ready to share with his readers the message he had received from Jesus: that God is light and in Him there is no darkness at all (v. 5). We have no record that Jesus made the statement, "God is Light" specifically to the apostle but that basic message had been conveyed to His followers during His earthly ministry. What does "God is light" mean? God is so pure and holy and His illuminating presence so real and bright that darkness cannot reside where He is. When God comes into the life of a person, the sin and darkness once there must leave. Just as darkness flees when a person turns on a light in a room, so darkness in one's life flees when God's illuminating power floods the believing heart.

B. God forgives (vv. 7-10).

John affirms that those who walk in the light are cleansed from sin. Does this mean believers will live a sinless and perfect life? Not at all. But when we do fall, and we certainly will, John declares that the "blood of Jesus Christ [will] cleanse us from all sin" (v. 7b, NKJV). And, just to clarify his point (that believers will sin), he denies the Gnostic heresy which held that we don't have any principle of sin within us. "If we say that we have no sin, we deceive ourselves, and the truth is not in us" (v. 8).

This does not give us license to sin at will and claim, "Well, the Bible affirms that we are sinners, so I'm just going by what the Bible says." John wants his readers to know that we have a sin nature that is constantly battling our spiritual person. Paul tells us that when we would do good, evil is always present (see Romans 7:7-25). So, to say that we are free from our sin nature is not true, according to John. And, as a result, our sin nature may cause us to do things which are against God's Word. But, "if we confess our sins [God] is faithful and just to forgive us [our sins] and to cleanse us from all unrighteousness" (v. 9, NKJV).

C. God cleanses (2:1-2).

John concludes this portion of his letter to his "little children" by informing them of his purpose for writing: to encourage them not to sin. However, if they do sin, they need not worry about losing right standing with God. In fact, they have an "advocate", a *parak-*

letos' (Greek), which means called to be at one's side. Jesus had said that the *parakletos* was the Holy Spirit (see John 14:26). But John tells the church that the Advocate is Jesus Christ.

Just as an attorney is called to represent a client in a courtroom, John affirms that Jesus represents believers before God and acts as their counselor. So, as we confess our sins, Jesus is there to act in our behalf, providing the basis for the Father to forgive us and restore us back to our place of fellowship. And why? John tells the church that Jesus is the "propitiation" for our sins. Propitiation means an atoning sacrifice, the means for blotting out sin. Jesus' death on the cross became the means by which we were made righteous. He was the living sacrifice and His blood atoned for the sins of all humankind.

3. John's exhortation of abiding (vv. 3-6)

John had been leading up to his main point in this section of his letter by laying the necessary groundwork to refute the Gnostics' understanding of knowledge. They believed that "knowledge" of God had to do with some mystical experience or direct vision from the divine. Their belief was that knowledge was purely religious attainment and had nothing to do with moral behavior. But John makes it clear that only those who keep God's commandment can claim they "know God". Jesus made a similar statement by telling His disciples, "If anyone loves Me, he will keep My word; and My Father will love him, and We will come to him and make Our home with him" (John 14:23, NKJV). So, mystical experiences are not evidence that one "knows" God. On the contrary, if one does not obey God and claim they "know" Him, they are liars and out of touch with the truth of His Word.

However, those who desire to keep God's Word and allow it to abide in their hearts have access to Him. Also, a believer's love for God will be made complete in his/her life. Therefore, those who acknowledge that they "know" God and abide in His presence must live as Jesus did. While John does not give specifics as to how Jesus lived, his Gospel describes how Jesus laid down His life for a friend and died on the cross for us.

Though God is concerned with our church attendance, He is more concerned with the love we show to one another. When we live as Jesus did, God's love will be complete and mature in us so that we can keep His commandments and help others do the same.

DISCERNING MY DUTY

1. *Why was John concerned about giving his "little children" knowledge from God?*
2. *What did he mean by God's love being "perfected" in believers? How can we know that God's love is perfected in us?*
3. *Since we have a sin nature how can we keep from sinning? Explain.*

DECIDING MY RESPONSE

To think about—Is there someone you have a hard time loving? After studying this lesson, and understanding how to perfect God's love in you, be prepared to put "love in action" by sacrificing your time, talents and treasures for the person.

To do—Reflect this week on John's words of "abiding" and "love." Give consideration as to how to remain in fellowship with God and other believers based on the lesson. Share your feelings with others during the week.

WHAT I WILL DO

_____

_____

LIGHT ON THE HEAVY

Propitiation: 2:2—Means a provision for pity or mercy. "Without propitiation, God would be saying, Sin may be ignored.'" With the propitiation in the blood of Christ, God is saying, "This is what your sin cost me, and I bore it in my Son, as I justified you." *(Zondervan's Pictorial Bible Dictionary,* p. 690).

Advocate: 2:1—One who supports, helps, speaks in behalf of. Fellowship: 1:6 That which is held in common. Heavenly love which fills the hearts of believers for one another and God.

Fellowship: 1:6—That which is held in common. Heavenly love which fills the hearts of believers for one another and God.

Knowing and Abiding

DEFINING THE ISSUE

There's an old saying, "To know me is to love me." In other words one must spend time getting to know a person to determine whether one loves another. It is this spending time, or abiding, that makes the difference.

As we abide in the presence of another, we get to know that person and grow to love him or her. So it is with God. We can't really "know" Him unless we abide in His presence.

The Gnostics in the Apostle John's day believed that knowledge was superior to love and/or virtue. However, their definition of knowledge was a mystical experience that only a few could attain. God is not interested in only a few people knowing Him. His desire is for all His created beings to know and abide in His presence that He might be acknowledged as Lord of all and fulfill His perfect purposes through them.

Various cults and pseudo-religions have denied Jesus Christ as Lord simply because they refuse to abide in His presence and love. Regardless of the various philosophies that may be shaping the minds of our modern world, Jesus Christ remains the Way, the Truth, and the Life. No one can "know" God and eventually become a citizen of the kingdom of heaven, unless he or she confesses that Jesus is Lord over his or her life.

The Apostle John in his First Epistle warns his "little children" regarding the various antichristian spirits in the first century. These warnings shouldn't be taken lightly in the 20th century. After all, the same spirit is trying to overtake the church today. We must be on guard so we won't be deceived by philosophies, man-made traditions, or other "forces" that try to lead us away from the simple message of the Gospel of the Lord Jesus Christ.

AIM

By the end of the session participants should:
1. *Know what is meant by false doctrines.*
2. *Become convinced they should be alert for false teaching,*
3. *Take steps to fortify themselves against false doctrines.*

SCRIPTURE TEXT

1 JOHN 2:18 Little children, it is the last time: and as ye have heard that antichrist shall come, even now are there many antichrists; whereby we know that it is the last time.

19 They went out from us, but they were not of us; for if they had been of us, they would no doubt have continued with us: but they went out, that they might be made manifest that they were not all of us.

20 But ye have an unction from the Holy One, and ye know all things.

21 I have not written unto you, because ye know not the truth, but because ye know it, and that no lie is of the truth.

22 Who is a liar but he that denieth that Jesus is the Christ? He is antichrist, that denieth the Father and the Son.

23 Whosoever denieth the Son, the same hath not the Father: [but] he that acknowledgeth the Son hath the Father also.

24 Let that therefore abide in you, which ye have heard from the beginning. If that which ye have heard from the beginning shall remain in you, ye also shall continue in the Son, and in the Father.

25 And this is the promise that he hath promised us, even eternal life.

26 These things have I written unto you concerning them that seduce you.

27 But the anointing which ye have received of him abideth in you, and ye need not that any man teach you: but as the same anointing teacheth you of all things, and is truth, and is no lie, and even as it hath taught you, ye shall abide in him.

28 And now, little children, abide in him; that, when he shall appear, we may have confidence, and not be ashamed before him at his coming.

29 If ye know that he is righteous, ye know that every one that doeth righteousness is born of him.

BIBLE BACKGROUND

The Apostle John wrote to the first century church sometime in the late 80s or early 90s. Some scholars believe John wrote the epistles after he wrote the Gospel and before the persecution under Domitian in 95. The epistle is written in sermon style to Christians all over Asia Minor.

John wrote as a parent would to his "little children" (1 John 2:1), because he was concerned about their spiritual welfare. He wanted the church to have a strong foundation and knowledge of the Spirit. John set the tone for the church so they would seek knowledge in certain areas. But the knowledge to which John referred didn't originate with human understanding. The knowledge to which he referred came as a result of "an unction from the Holy One" (1 John 2:20). As the church received the anointing, they also had the knowledge to abide in God's presence which would give them power to overcome the works of the wicked one, or Antichrist.

POINTS TO PONDER

1. *According to the Apostle John who is coming during the last hour?*
2. *How would the church know the people with the antichristian spirit?*
3. *John declares emphatically that the person who lies is one that does what?*
4. *How can one have confidence?*
5. *Those that practice righteousness are actually born of whom?*

THE LESSON AT-A-GLANCE

1. *Beware of the Antichrists (1 John 2:18-20)*
2. *Abide in the Truth (vv. 21-26)*
3. *Abide in God (vv. 27-29)*

EXPLORING THE MEANING
1. Beware of the Antichrists (1 John 2:18-20)

The Apostle John is older and more mature than the church he is addressing. Therefore, he identifies them as his "little children."

Since possibly he wrote the epistles after the Gospel, he perhaps desired to warn the young Christians of the events that were about to take place.

John seems to think that the church is living in the "last hour" of the present age and that a new age would soon appear. This new age would be when Jesus Christ made His second appearance. It is not clear how John concluded that the church was in its last hour (v. 18). But, what is more important is the apostle's warning that the Antichrist is coming. John says there were people in the community of faith that had the spirit of the Antichrist which lent credence to his point about the "last hour."

The apostle does not identify the Antichrist. But Morris states it is an idea or person in history that denies that Jesus is God; refutes the revelation of the Gospels; and completely rejects all that God has to offer. The "Antichrist" spirit is a false idea, a heresy, a lie. Whoever these people were, John warned the church that this spirit had crept in because it resided in people who had swallowed a lie about God—hook, line and sinker.

John tells the church that certain of the people with an antichristian spirit were at one time a part of the fellowship of the Johannine community. However, John is sure that if they were true Christians they would have remained a part of the community and not given in to the antichristian spirit. Just by going out of the church, i.e., breaking fellowship with the others, proved that these people did not belong to the household of faith (v. 19). Once they left the church, their true intentions became known to all. On the other hand, those who remained in the church would be given revelation knowledge so they would be able to identify these people and not associate with them.

Where does revelation knowledge come from? John said that it had come from an unction or "charisma", which is translated as "anointing" from the Lord. As a result the believers had access to knowledge of the Spirit. Unlike Gnosticism, which said knowledge is for an elite few, the anointing is for the purpose of imparting knowledge to all believers from above.

2. Abiding in the Truth (vv. 21-26)
John shows the church that truth and lies are not the same. A liar is one who refuses to believe that Jesus is the Christ, the anointed

One. Those who deny the divine nature of Christ according to John, have the spirit of the Antichrist.

John is clearly attacking the Docetic heresy rampant in the first century community at the time of his writing. Followers of Docetism believed that humanity and divinity could not reside in the same body. Consequently, Jesus Christ could not have been both human and God. But John tells the church that those who fall for the Docetic doctrine are liars simply because it renounced the truth about the Son of God.

If the church remained in union with Christ Jesus and the Father, they had the promise of eternal life (1 John 2:25). John had earlier shared the same message (see 1 John 1:2). The apostle also reaffirmed his reason for writing the church: To warn them about those who had the antichristian spirit that were trying to get people to stray from the truth.

3. Abiding in God (vv. 27-29)

John returns to one of his main points in the text. The Holy Spirit, with which each believer has been anointed, is a Teacher. He brings all things to a believer's remembrance. The Spirit illuminates and helps believers abide in Christ and in the Father so he or she will not fall victim to the rampant heresy in the community.

The apostle clearly affirms that the same Spirit of the living God that taught Jesus would do the same for believers who remained steadfast in the truth. The Holy Spirit does not lie or practice deceit like the Antichrists. Instead, He teaches and guides God's people into truth (see John 16:13), so they will not be led astray by false teachings.

Finally, John reminds his "little children" to abide in God (v. 28). Whenever Jesus returns, those who are "abiding" will have confidence that they will go home to be with the Lord because they have rejected the lies of society and held onto the Word of truth taught to them by the Holy Spirit.

John reminded the church, "If you know that He is righteous, you know that everyone who practices righteousness is born of Him" (v. 29, NKJV). There is an old saying: "If it looks like a duck, quacks like a duck, and swims like a duck, chances are it's a duck." Since God is righteous, those who live like Him are born of the Spirit.

John is calling the church to maturity in the Lord. He does not want them to be influenced by the society in which they live. That call is the same for us today. With the power of television, radio, newspapers, magazines, movies, and other media, it is easy to get sidetracked and influenced by the world's standard of thinking and living, and lose our heritage and fellowship with Him. However, God has poured out the Holy Spirit on His people that we might receive the anointing and discern what is good and true.

Mature believers remain on the cutting edge of society and help those who haven't experienced a relationship with Jesus Christ to know what it means to be saved. They share their experience and knowledge so others can know the truth and want to be followers of Christ. And yes, mature believers should seek to help those who may be trapped in cults and sects understand the basic message of the Gospel. "For God so loved the world, that He gave His only begotten Son that whosoever believes in Him should not perish but have everlasting life" (John 3:16). That truth will stand forever no matter what other doctrines may come our way.

DISCERNING MY DUTY

1. *Is John's concern for this church legitimate? Why?*
2. *How can we help those who are caught up in cults, sects, and false doctrine know the truth of the Christian faith?*
3. *How can we help persons who are teaching unscriptural traditions instead of the Gospel, teach the Word of God?*
4. *What false doctrines are making inroads in our churches and communities that are influencing us and our young people? What can we do to combat these forces?*

DECIDING MY RESPONSE

As you reflect on this lesson, devise an evangelistic plan to reach various people with the basic message of the Gospel. Report to the class or group next time you meet.

WHAT I WILL DO

_____

_____

LIGHT ON THE HEAVY

Unction—1 John 2:20, 27. In all three New Testament occurrences, unction and anointing are synonymous. Christians who, by virtue of their unction are able to discern schism and heresy. Grammatically "unction" must be either (a) that which is smeared on or (b) the act of anointing; but in either case the word refers to the gift of the Holy Spirit. *(The New Bible Dictionary,* 2nd ed., 1982, p. 1230).

The Difference Love Makes

DEFINING THE ISSUE

In a tenement in uptown New York City two conversations were occurring at the same time in different apartments. The first was between John and Natalie. John had just returned from a business trip, the third one in a month. He and Natalie were bickering about his time away from home.

"I hate it, John. And I hate you for accepting that position. You leave me alone week after week. What do you think I am, a doormat that you can walk over? Someone you can take for granted? I hate you for that!"

Over in the next apartment, Craig and Tanya were having the following conversation.

"Tanya, I love you so much. You mean the world to me. I would never do anything to hurt you. I would never leave you alone. This neighborhood is so unsafe. I would die if anything happened to you while we were apart. I hope you love me as much as I love you!"

Both couples were sharing their emotions. One of love, the other of hate. Poets, scientists, sociologists, doctors, and others have tried to define what love and hate really mean. Human love and hate are usually expressed with emotions. And, contrary to what many people believe, both love and hate derive from the same source. That is, humanly speaking, one usually doesn't love someone unless one cares for the person. And, one usually doesn't hate another unless at a previous time one cared or had a relationship with another which was injured.

One may wonder how a person who hates another can care for him or her. In the same respect, love emanates from emotions that have developed over time. One cannot care about another unless he or she loves that person. So, in some instances there is a thin line between love and hate.

God's desire, is that we love every day. When we do, we are able to overcome hatred, malice, contempt, and any other emotions that can ruin our fellowship with Him and other people.

In this study John encourages the church to conduct itself in love and stay away from hating others. Though it may be a tall order to fulfill, God has the power to help us accomplish His will. All we need to do is ask and trust Him to show us how.

AIM

By the end of the study the participants will:
1. *Understand the nature of true love.*
2. *Feel the need of expressing true love to others.*
3. *Decide to show true love to another person in some tangible action.*

SCRIPTURE TEXT

1 JOHN 3:11 For this is the message that ye heard from the beginning, that we should love one another.

12 Not as Cain, who was of that wicked one, and slew his brother. And wherefore slew he him? Because his own works were evil, and his brother's righteous.

13 Marvel not, my brethren, if the world hate you.

14 We know that we have passed from death unto life, because we love the brethren. He that loveth not his brother abideth in death.

15 Whosoever hateth his brother is a murderer: and ye know that no murderer hath eternal life abiding in him.

16 Hereby perceive we the love of God, because he laid down his life for us: and we ought to lay down our lives for the brethren.

17 But whoso hath this world's good, and seeth his brother have need, and shutteth up his bowels of compassion from him, how dwelleth the love of God in him?

18 My little children, let us not love in word, neither in tongue; but in deed and in truth.

19 And hereby we know that we are of the truth, and shall assure our hearts before him.

20 For if our heart condemn us, God is greater than our heart, and knoweth all things.

21 Beloved, if our heart condemn us not, then have we confidence toward God.

22 And whatsoever we ask, we receive of him, because we keep his commandments, and do those things that are pleasing in his sight.

23 And this is his commandment, That we should believe on the name of his Son Jesus Christ, and love one another, as he gave us commandment.

24 And he that keepeth his commandments dwelleth in him, and he in him. And hereby we know that he abideth in us, by the Spirit which he hath given us.

BIBLE BACKGROUND

John continues his teaching to the church regarding the life of Jesus Christ and their position in Him. Last week, we learned from the apostle that an antichristian spirit was trying to run rampant in the community and the church, a false teaching which denied the lordship of Jesus and His Oneness with the Father.

John comforted the church with his words about the anointing of the Holy Spirit which had been given to them as a result of their relationship with Jesus. Now the apostle is prepared to show the church how to put the love of God into action. This love has been shed abroad by the Holy Spirit in their hearts and manifests itself by the way we treat others.

POINTS TO PONDER

1. *What is the basic message John shares with the people?*
2. *According to John, why did Cain murder his brother, Abel?*
3. *If someone claims he or she is a Christian yet hates another Christian what does this mean?*
4. *How are we to display love?*
5. *What is the most basic commandment to which we should adhere?*

THE LESSON AT-A-GLANCE

1. Love, don't hate (1 John 3:11-15)
2. Put love into action (vv. 16-18)
3. Love abides in the truth (vv. 19-24)

EXPLORING THE MEANING

1. Love, don't hate (1 John 3:11-15)

The true test of discipleship and sonship is that we practice righteousness and have love for one another (see 1 John 3: 11). No one can claim to be God-like if he or she does not have love for another child of God. After all, Jesus told His disciples: "A new command I give you: Love one another. As I have loved you, so you must love one another. All men will know that you are my disciples if you love one another" (John 13:34-35, NIV). Therefore, John declares that the Christian community has heard this message, perhaps from various sources and certainly from himself, since the beginning of his ministry. They are to love one another.

The apostle reminds the church that their attitude should not be like that of Cain, one of Adam's sons who murdered his brother Abel, while they were out in the field (Genesis 4:8-10). Cain's actions were motivated by jealousy and the spirit of the devil, "who was a murderer from the beginning" (John 8:44c, NKJV). John sees Cain's works as evil, while Abel's works were considered righteous because the Lord "looked with favor on Abel and his offering" (Genesis 4:4b, NIV).

We must carefully guard our hearts from envy and jealousy against other people. God knows what each of us needs and desires. As He blesses someone with material or spiritual goods, He expects us to rejoice with them. We should thank God that His blessings are available to all His children. After all, the Word tells us that He shows no partiality toward people (see Acts 10:34). He will fulfull His purpose for each of us as we surrender ourselves to Him. Therefore, we have no business being jealous or envious of other Christians. They are our brothers and sisters too.

John's readers may have been confused and frightened that the world hated them because of their love for Christ. But he tells them not to marvel or be astounded by the world's hatred. Jesus had told His disciples the same thing when He prayed to the Father: "I have given them Your word; and the world has hated them because they are not of the world, just as I am not of the world" (John 17:14, NKJV). So John admonishes the church to be steadfast in the face of opposition toward them. And, regarding our love for one another, the apostle affirms that one who has passed from spiritual death to spiritual life is one who loves his/her brethren.

In contrast, one who does not love a fellow Christian is in spiritual darkness which is, in reality, death. One cannot claim to be spiritual without having love for his/her brother or sister. Since God is love and Jesus Christ is the manifestation of love, how can we abide in Him without loving others? As far as John is concerned those who do not love are spiritually dead. He even goes one step further by saying, "Anyone who hates his brother is a murderer" (l John 3: 15, NIV).

2. Put love into action (w. 16-18)

After painting a vivid picture of hatred and murder, John turns to a positive thought by reminding the church about the nature of true love. God, in the form of Jesus, willingly died on the cross, i.e., "laid down his life" for us (see John 15:13). No greater love can be displayed toward others than for one to sacrifice his/her life for another. And, while we know that Jesus' death is the means for our salvation, John suggests that Christians ought to be willing to sacrifice their time, talents and treasure, for the good of someone else, just as Jesus did.

That's really putting love in action. Love is more than mere "lip service." We cannot really love another without doing something for another. A wife would have a hard time believing a husband loves her unless he shows her love on a consistent basis. A child would have a difficult time believing that his/her parents love him/her if they never showed it.

True love is based on a decision that is manifested in action. If love is based solely on "feelings," not much action will take place, especially if those feelings change.

3. Love abides in the truth (w. 19-24)

John continues his exhortation by stating that those who are of the truth actually love in deed. As a result of our actions we can be sure that our hearts are in right standing with the Lord. However,

John also wants the church to know that if their hearts do condemn them, God is greater than their hearts and knows all things. It could be that, though we want to love in deed and actions, our conscience may convict us of times when we have failed. But, according to the apostle, we needn't worry about that. God knows who we are, what our motives are and whether we really love others.

We are human and prone to make mistakes. Therefore, we shouldn't condemn ourselves to the point that we become spiritually "paralyzed." God knows our hearts and our very thoughts before we even think them. In contrast, if our conscience condemns us, we should be thankful that the Lord loves us so much He is willing to "chastise us" (see Hebrews 12:5).

In the same sense, if our hearts do not condemn us, i.e., if we have no unconfessed sins in our lives, then we can come boldly before God with our petitions. John calls this having "confidence toward God" (1 John 3:21).

John reminds the church that have confidence toward God, whatever they ask, in prayer, in the name of Jesus, shall be received from Him. Of course, this does not mean we can pray for wild and frivolous things that oppose His will and expect to receive them. What John means is that those who keep God's commandments of loving and serving Him by serving others, can expect God to bless them as they pray according to His perfect will (see 1 John 3:22). John also reminds the church that God's commandment is simple to understand. We must believe that Jesus Christ is the Son of God and the only means for salvation, and love others as we love Him (see Matthew 22:37-39). Certainly, our belief in Jesus Christ as the Saviour of the world ought to be displayed in acts of service for others, since Jesus has commanded us to do so.

Finally, the apostle returns to a familiar point of abiding in God. Those who keep His commandments "abide" in Him and He in them. Abiding means to reside in a certain place. Thus, the apostle makes it clear that those who are in Christ, and He in them, know it because of the indwelling of the Holy Spirit.

Love is a powerful force in the universe. Our responsibility is to share God's love with others who may need to know what His love is all about. After all, God has given us the commandment to love others as He has loved us. We can't afford not to.

DISCERNING MY DUTY

1. *What does John mean when he says "marvel not" if the world hates you? How does the world display its hatred toward Christians?*
2. *Compare 1 John 3:17 with James 2:15-17. What do these passages of Scripture seem to be saying to the early churches and to us today?*
3. *Based on John's writings a Christian is one who loves. Does that mean we are to love everyone, including those who desire to hurt us? Explain.*

DECIDING MY RESPONSE

To think about—Discuss what the church can do to promote love and unity in a world that seems to be torn by strife, hatred and confusion. Are there answers to these problems, and if so, should the church or the government be leading the way to solve them?

To do—As you reflect on today's lesson think of someone you may have difficulty loving. Take steps to share: (1) the lesson with him or her; and (2) something that will cost you, in time or finances, with the person. Be prepared to share your testimony with the class next week.

WHAT I WILL DO

_____

_____

LIGHT ON THE HEAVY

Cain—The eldest son of Adam and Eve, at whose birth Eve said, "I have gotten a man" (see Genesis 4:1). He was an agriculturalist—unlike Abel, who was a shepherd-and was "of the evil one" (see 1 John 3:12). Out of harmony with God, Cain's offering was rejected, and he subsequently killed his brother (Genesis 4:8). God punished him by sending him to become a wanderer, perhaps a nomad in the land of Nod, and to protect him from being slain God set a mark on him.

Parallels to the conflict between Cain and Abel have been drawn from Sumerian literature, where disputations concerning the relative merits of agriculture and herding are found, but in none of those known does the farmer kill the herdsman, and such a conflict probably only reflects the historical situation in Mesopotamia from late prehistoric times onwards. *(New Bible Dictionary,* 2nd ed., 1982, p. 157).

Fear and Love

DEFINING THE ISSUE

Most of us know something about love. A popular song from a few years ago had the following lyrics: "I'll do anything for you. Anything you want me to, I'll do. I'll go anywhere with you. Anywhere you want me to go, I'll go. I'll be anything for you. Anything you want me to be, I'll be." What the songwriter seemed to convey is that love will cause one to do anything, go anywhere, and be anything for another, regardless of the cost.

Fear also is something all of us are familiar with. When we are fearful of things, we tend to shy away and want no part of them regardless of the cost.

One of the reasons husbands and wives have disagreements is because the husband may be insensitive to the wife's fear of certain things. However, because of her love for him she is willing to be involved with him regardless of her personal uncertainties. For example, a wife may fear high speed rollercoasters. Because she loves her husband, however, she may ride them just to be with him.

Certainly, we can relate to fear. Fear can paralyze a person and keep him/her from being his/her best in a given situation. But God does not want us to be needlessly fearful. He has promised in His Word that He will be with us always (Matthew 28:20), and He has not given us a spirit of fear (see 2 Timothy 1:7). Just as God's love can empower us for service, it can also break the power of fear in us.

As we allow the love of God to fill our hearts, the resulting faith and power can enable us to be victorious over fear, doubt, confusion, and any other negative feelings we may have.

In this Scripture text John gives practical applications to his "little children" that they may love others and in the process drive out any fear that may be within.

AIM

By the end of the study, the participants should:

1. *Know how to trust God in fearful times*
2. *Sense God's readiness to make us secure because of His love*
3. *Determine to rely on Him when fear comes.*

SCRIPTURE TEXT

1 JOHN 4:7 Beloved, let us love one another: for love is of God; and every one that loveth is born of God, and knoweth God.

8 He that loveth not knoweth not God; for God is love.

9 In this was manifested the love of God toward us, because that God sent his only begotten Son into the world, that we might live through him.

10 Herein is love, not that we loved God, but that he loved us, and sent his Son to be the propitiation for our sins.

11 Beloved, if God so loved us, we ought also to love one another.

12 No man hath seen God at any time. If we love one another, God dwelleth in us, and his love is perfected in us.

13 Hereby know we that we dwell in him, and he in us, because he hath given us of his Spirit.

14 And we have seen and do testify that the Father sent the Son to be the Saviour of the world.

15 Whosoever shall confess that Jesus is the Son of God, God dwelleth in him, and he in God.

16 And we have known and believed the love that God hath to us. God is love; and he that dwelleth in love dwelleth in God, and God in him.

17 Herein is our love made perfect, that we may have boldness in the day of judgment: because as he is, so are we in this world.

18 There is no fear in love; but perfect love casteth out fear: because fear hath torment. He that feareth is not made perfect in love.

19 We love him, because he first loved us.

20 If a man say, I love God, and hateth his brother, he is a liar: for he that loveth not his brother whom he hath seen, how can he love God whom he hath not seen?

21 And this commandment have we from him, That he who loveth God love his brother also.

BIBLE BACKGROUND

The Apostle John continues his exhortation with the first century Christian community. The last lesson dealt with love and hate. John warns the church that those who claim they are Christians must love others just as Christ has loved them.

As we begin today's lesson John has just warned the church not to believe every spirit. Instead he wants them to "try the spirits whether they are of God: because many false prophets are gone out into the world" (1 John 4:1). Gnosticism and Docetism were rampant. Docetism denied that Jesus had come in the flesh, which was in direct opposition to the teachings of John. Therefore, the apostle makes it clear: "And every spirit that does not confess that Jesus Christ has come in the flesh is not of God. And this is the spirit of the antichrist, which you have heard was coming, and is now already in the world" (1 John 4:3, NKJV).

He continues to admonish his readers to hold to the truth of the Gospel. Those who hear what John has to say regarding the truth are of God. Those that refuse the truth cannot be of God or of the true Church. As we begin, John clearly defines how one can tell if he or she is of God.

POINTS TO PONDER

1. *What is one of the requirements for knowing God?*
2. *How did God show His love toward His children?*
3. *For what purpose may God's love be perfected or matured in us?*
4. *When God's love is perfected in us, what will be one of its results?*

THE LESSON AT-A-GLANCE

1. *God's love shown toward His children (1 John 4:7-12)*
2. *God's love abides in His children (vv. 13-16)*
3. *God's love relieves fear (vv. 17-21)*

EXPLORING THE MEANING
1. God's love shown toward His children (1 John 4:7-12)

John starts by calling the church "beloved." He assumes that those who are part of the community have followed the standard set before them regarding loving one another (see 1 John 3:11). However, John is quick to remind them to love one another, because love is "of God" and everyone who loves is born of God and knows God.

The apostle says that love is a divine characteristic of God. It was best displayed at the cross of Calvary. The Apostle Paul tells us that "God showed his great love for us by sending Christ to die for us while we were still sinners" (Romans 5:8, LB). Therefore, believers in Jesus Christ will not only love others but display that fruit in their lives. Only a Christian can really love as God has, i.e., sacrificing our own interests for the interests of others (see 1 John 3:16).

The world is selfish and motivated by a "me first" philosophy that leaves little room for God's way of thinking. Many people wouldn't even consider sacrificing their agenda for others. Yet that is exactly what God admonishes us to do. The apostle makes this emphatic point: people who do not love in the way He has challenged us to, don't even know Him.

We've heard the old saying that "he's a chip off the old block" in referring to a son who resembles his father. So it is with Christians. We must be loving and caring for others just as God is with us. How can we really know God intimately if we don't display His basic nature and characteristics? When the apostle says, "God is love" (v. 8), he means that God's nature and makeup are of love. Every thought, motive and action of God springs from love. How can we really be followers of Him without aspiring to be the same?

John clarifies how God's love is displayed toward people. He has almost repeated John 3:16 concerning the love of God: "He sent his only begotten Son into the world, that we might live through him" (1 John 3:9). Only by accepting the death of Jesus Christ as our way of salvation can we really experience the love of God. Since it was *agape* love that emanated from the Cross, the apostle is describing God's love as the self-giving, self-sacrificing kind that always seeks the best in others.

John affirms a basic truth when he says: "No one has seen God at any time" (v. 12). This is a familiar truth that John has presented before (see John 1:18), and probably something the church knew through experience. Nevertheless, since the community has not seen the Son, how can they know who God is? He is manifested through the lives of those who love Him and have allowed His love to mature in them. Since we are instruments of God's divine peace and love, we must also show the world we are born of God through the various acts of love and service we give others. Some people may have never set foot in a church or opened a Bible, but they can get to know God and His love for them by how we treat them. If we are born of God, we must love.

2. God's love abides in His children (vv. 13-16)

John has clarified the essence and nature of love so his readers wouldn't be ignorant of it. In keeping with an earlier point he made (see 1 John 3:24b), the apostle affirms that the way to know whether we abide in God and He in us is through the Holy Spirit. When the Holy Spirit controls our lives, we are able to give love, and be patient with others. The Spirit of God comforts and brings things to our remembrance so that we can live victoriously in Him.

John continues by stating, "we have seen and testify that the Father has sent the Son as Saviour of the world" (v. 14, NKJV). It would appear that by "we" the apostle is referring to the disciples who walked and talked with Jesus, which he mentioned previously (see 1 John 1:1-4). However, Morris indicates that John is referring to the whole church community because of their abiding faith in God, rather than the original eyewitnesses of Jesus' earthly ministry. Whatever the case, John wants his readers to know that "whoever confesses that Jesus is the Son of God" (1 John 3:15) has God in him/her and He in them.

3. God's love relieves fear (vv. 17-21)

John proceeds to explain how the love of God, which has been given to us, can be matured. Once we allow God's love to control our lives, it will grow and become complete. As a result we will be able to come boldly before God's throne of judgment, confident that He will not cast us away. Why? John tells us that because we have lived as Jesus did we needn't worry that God will reject us in the day of judgment.

This does not mean that we will live a sinless and perfect life as Jesus did. However, God knows each heart and is aware of those whose motives have been pure while working to bring His kingdom into reality. At the day of judgment everyone's works will be revealed. If our hearts have been right, God will say, "Well done, thou good and faithful servant . . . enter thou into the joy of thy Lord" (Matthew 25:21).

Love will be perfect and complete in believers on the day of judgment. Furthermore we can be assured that God's love, given to a believer today, casts out the fear of His judgments. Love and fear of God cannot reside in us at the same time. The apostle says that fear involves torment (1 John 3:18), and it is not God's will that any of His children be tormented by anything. If one is being tormented by the fear of God, His love has not been matured in him or her.

Finally, the apostle returns to a now-familiar thought. We are motivated to love God because of His love shown toward us. But, how can we really love God? By showing love toward our brothers and sisters. According to John, if someone says, "I love God" and hates his/her brother or sister, then he/she is lying about his/her love for God. After all, we certainly can't hate God's children, whom we see and interact with every day, and love Him. The thoughts are inconsistent. Jesus Christ has given us the commandment to love one another even as He has loved us. The apostle reminds the church of the same notion as he concludes this part of his letter (see v. 21).

Love is not an option for the Christian. We are commanded to love others even as Jesus has loved us. Our love will drive out any fear of God in us because we will know that we are doing the Master's will.

DISCERNING MY DUTY

1. *Is fear a healthy emotion to have? Discuss.*
2. *Why is it important to allow God's love to mature in us?*
3. *How can we be sure we are operating in God's love? Explain.*

DECIDING MY RESPONSE

To think about Often in our world, people are fearful because of their circumstances. What charitable organizations can we support to show our compassion for people who are fearful because they have AIDS? Because they are homeless? Because they are unwed mothers?

To do Are there times you may be fearful of God and other people? Based on today's lesson, reflect on ways you can break that fear. Remember to thank God for His unfailing love shown toward you even in your weakest moments. Prepare to share with the class the following week.

WHAT I WILL DO

_____

_____

LIGHT ON THE HEAVY

Propitiate; Propitiation (1 John 4:10)—The removal of wrath by the offering of a gift. This may be a crude process of appeasement or bribery, or it may denote something much more refined and spiritual. Granted, words like propitiation and wrath are not ideal ones to describe God's activities. However, propitiation does not mean that God is bribed to be gracious; the removal of His wrath is due to Himself alone (see Leviticus 17:11; Psalm 78:38). But it is really wrath that is removed. There are four important New Testment passages regarding propitiation: Romans 3:25, Hebrews 2:17, 1 John 2:22 and 4:10. Each of these passages puts forward the thought that God's opposition to sin is more than token. Christ is the answer; He provides the means of averting divine wrath. It is this that the New Testament writers have in mind when they speak of propitiation. *(The International Standard Bible Encyclopedia,* Vol. 3, 1986, pp.1004-1005.)

Faith and Life

DEFINING THE ISSUE

Today, it seems that more and more people are trying to fill a spiritual void in their lives. As a result various cults and pseudo-religious groups are cropping up with the promise to fill that void. Satan is on the prowl for the young and old alike.

The temptation to have a life full of power, fortune, and fame has blinded many to believe these things will fill that spiritual void. Also, for many the desire for material comfort has replaced the felt need for spiritual fulfillment.

Many people have no idea that their inward yearning is actually to be in concert with God. Instead of turning to Him, they seek fulfillment in "things." Unfortunately, some people have committed suicide after being involved in cults, or losing their material possessions, because their life's hopes were built around things instead of God.

A fulfilling and abundant life must be centered in Jesus Christ. Not only can He fill any void in our lives, He gives us eternal life which begins the moment we receive Him and continues when our earthly journey is over. This week John will help us see what it means to have faith in Christ. It's a message we can appreciate ourselves. It's also a truth which we can share with those who are trapped in various cults and with material possessions. God wants to set them free!

AIM

By the end of the session:

1. *Participants will discover the meaning and significance of Jesus Christ*
2. *Will sense the desireability of a life of faith*
3. *Will commit to pursuing a deeper life of trust in God, thanking Him for what He has already done to show His trustworthiness.*

SCRIPTURE TEXT

1 JOHN 5:1 Whosoever believeth that Jesus is the Christ is born of God: and every one that loveth him that begat loveth him also that is begotten of him.

2 By this we know that we love the children of God, when we love God, and keep his commandments.

3 For this is the love of God, that we keep his commandments: and his commandments are not grievous.

4 For whatsoever is born of God overcometh the world: and this is the victory that overcometh the world, even our faith.

5 Who is he that overcometh the world, but he that believeth that Jesus is the Son of God?

6 This is he that came by water and blood, even Jesus Christ; not by water only, but by water and blood. And it is the Spirit that beareth witness because the Spirit is truth.

7 For there are three that bear record in heaven, the Father, the Word, and the Holy Ghost: and these three are one.

8 And there are three that bear witness in earth, the Spirit, and the water, and the blood: and these three agree in one.

9 If we receive the witness of men, the witness of God is greater: for this is the witness of God which he hath testified of his Son.

10 He that believeth on the Son of God hath the witness in himself; he that believeth not God hath made him a liar; because he believeth not the record that God gave of his Son.

11 And this is the record, that God hath given to us eternal life, and this life is in his Son.

12 He that hath the Son hath life; and he that hath not the Son of God hath not life.

13 These things have I written unto you that believe on the name of the Son of God; that ye may know that ye have eternal life, and that ye may believe on the name of the Son of God.

BIBLE BACKGROUND

The community to whom John wrote his epistle is believed to have been in Asia. His purpose was to address the heresy of Gnosticism which was spreading rampantly in the first century community and threatening the truth of Jesus Christ upon which the community was built.

In the first epistle John uses a method of argumentation called deductive logic. This consists of some statements which serve as premises, or statements of evidence, and others which serve as the conclusions that can be drawn from the premises.

If we use the first three letters of the alphabet to represent particular statements, *deductive logic* would look like this: If statement A implies statement B, and if B implies C, then A will imply C *(World Book Encyclopedia,* Childcraft International, 1980, vol. 12, p. 381). Using this method, John presents his argument to the church based on logical reasoning.

The apostle encourages the church regarding their relationship with Jesus Christ. As a result believers: (1) have love for one another; (2) are obedient to God; (3) receive the power to overcome the world; and (4) receive eternal life.

POINTS TO PONDER

1. *What is one of the ways we love God?*
2. *How does one overcome the world?*
3. *Who bears the witness of Christ?*
4. *According to John how does one know he or she has eternal life?*
5. *Why did John write this letter to the church?*

THE LESSON AT-A-GLANCE

1. *Faith in Christ (1 John 5:1-5)*
2. *Witness in Christ (vv. 6-10)*
3. *Life through Christ (vv. 11-13)*

EXPLORING THE MEANING
1. Faith in Christ (1 John 5:1-5)

Our lesson begins with what is actually a continuation of John's line of reasoning developed in the latter part of Chapter 4. John had been talking about love for God and for others (1 John 4:19-21). In our present text he goes on to clarify the nature and results of love.

For John, "whosoever believeth that Jesus is the Christ is born of God" (1 John 5:1a). The "whosoever" acts as an open invitation to include those in and outside of the Christian community to whom the apostle is writing. It also includes everyone who reads these words over time and accepts the evidence presented to them.

The word "believes" means to adhere to, trust in, and rely on the truths presented. It is more than just "head knowledge." It includes putting the belief into action. Therefore, one must readily accept, *and act on the fact* that Jesus the Christ, the anointed One, and the promised Messiah are one and the same. This is how we know that we are "born again." At the same time, those who are united with God through Jesus Christ, not only love Him ("Him that begat"), but also love His children ("him also that is begotten of Him"). We are joint heirs with Christ and brothers and sisters to each other in God's spiritual family. How we relate to one another is a reflection of our relationship to God.

Here's how one can tell whether one loves God's children: if we love God and keep His commandments. One might wonder whether John has turned this truth around so that it reads incorrectly. But he is emphasizing a previous point he made (see 1 John 3:23) as well as a statement Jesus had made to His disciples (see John 13:34). So, John's concept is not erroneous. One cannot truly love God without loving His children or vice versa. And one cannot keep God's commandments without love (see John 14:15)!

One might also ask, what are the commandments we should keep? We should love God and love our neighbors as we love ourselves (see Luke 10:27). In John's view we are not asked to do something difficult ("and His commandments are not grievous," 1 John 5:3). As a matter of fact Jesus told His disciples, "My yoke is easy and My burden is light" (Matthew 11:30). So, if one is to love God, one will be able to love God's children because He has commanded that we do so, and God has empowered us to keep His commandment.

The reason God's commandments are not burdensome is that obedience to them enables us to overcome the world. Believers have been given the power by God to overcome the forces of temptation which would prevent our obedience. According to John, our faith in Christ enables us to overcome the world. And by believing, trusting, and adhering to the fact that Jesus is the Son of the living God, we are victorious over everything that is not like God. What in the world do we have to overcome? Spiritual, physical, and emotional forces that try to weigh us down. Black people encounter daily unique injustices on their jobs, in their neighborhoods, and from their government. How can they overcome these things? The key is to hold on to God's hand at all times. Too often we attempt to conquer our problems on our own and, as a result, cannot see beyond the situations we face. That is why John says, "whosoever is born of God" conquers.

John says that to believe Jesus is the Son of God and to be a member of the spiritual family of God enables one to overcome the world and its demonic systems. Interestingly, the victory is not the overcoming itself, but obtaining that which enables us to hold fast our faith. We should regard Jesus as our example, One who remained faithful to the end. Though He was wounded for our trangressions, He did not complain but willingly died on the cross that we might be saved.

2. Witness in Christ (vv. 6-10)

John continues his exhortation to the church by giving them a definitive description of Jesus, the One who came "by water and blood" (v. 6a). The phrase, "water and blood" could mean several things. One possibility is its reference to the elements that flowed from Jesus' side after His death on the cross (John 19:34). This seems to emphasize that Jesus Christ was human and He physically suffered just as anyone else would.

Another view is that it refers to Jesus' baptism by water in the Jordan River and His baptism by blood through His crucifixion. Still another view is that it refers to the sacraments of baptism and communion that we continue as a testimony to Christ.

If we consider the function of these elements, water and blood, we find that water is an essential constituent of many different substances as well as a necessity of life. It is also known for its cleansing ability. Blood is also a necessity of life that delivers oxygen and nutrients to every cell and tissue of the body as well as removes waste products. We might conclude that the phrase "water and blood" speaks of Jesus' redeeming power which cleanses and atones us. His water gives us everlasting life and His blood removes our sins. There is life through Jesus Christ.

John also tells the church that the Spirit bears witness to the very fact that Jesus came by water and blood because the "Spirit is truth" (1 John 5:6). This witness has firsthand knowledge of Jesus, which helps guide believers into all truth.

John continues by saying, "For there are three that bear record in heaven, the Father, the Word, and the Holy Ghost: and these three are one. And there are three that bear witness in earth. . . ." (vv. 7-8). These words did not belong to the original manuscript but are believed to have been marginal notes which later found their way into the text. The New International Version translates vv. 7-8 as follows: "For there are three that testify: the Spirit, the water and the blood; and the three are in agreement."

Legally, the witness of at least two persons was necessary to convict under the Mosaic Law. What John seems to be saying is that the three witnesses all "convict" us to the truth of Christ. The Spirit "convicts" us inwardly and our testimony by baptism and communion are outward forms of witnessing to the truth that Jesus is the Son of God.

For John, if one can receive the witness of human beings certainly we can receive the witness of God because His is greater than anyone else's. Those who believe in the Son of God have God's witness within them. The word "believe" is defined as the acceptance of something as true or real *(Doubleday Dictionary,* Doubleday and Company, Inc., 1975, p. 66). How one regards the source of that "something" determines whether or not it is accepted. Surely God's testimony carries more weight than what we say or do. And if we accept God's testimony, then we have the witness of the Spirit that is truth dwelling within us.

Anyone who does not accept God's truths is essentially saying that God's testimony is a lie and rejects the Spirit of truth. If we reject God's truths, we reject Him and have no part of His family.

3. Life through Christ (vv. 11-13)

Finally, the apostle proclaims that God has given us a record that we have eternal life in the Son of God. The word "record" is used to mean summon as witness, evidence or testimony. Eternal life gives testimony to everything that God has given us because it is found in Jesus Christ. Apparently some of the believers were having doubts about their relationships with God. To assure them John says, "These things I have written to you who believed in the name of the Son of God, that you may know that you have eternal life, and that you may continue to believe in the name of the Son of God" (v. 13, NKJV). Or perhaps they may have had "head knowledge" instead of "heart knowledge" of Jesus.

When one knows the truth, he or she lives in such a way that truth becomes a part of one's life. That is the most important aspect of John's words. We must have faith in Jesus Christ and allow that faith to become an integral part of our lives. As we continue in the truths of Jesus Christ, we have the assurance of eternal life even in the face of doubt and confusion. For John, and for us, this is the most important lesson we can learn about an abiding relationship with Jesus.

DISCERNING MY DUTY

1. *What are the implications if Jesus had come by water only?*

2. *Why did John make the distinction that Jesus is the Christ? Explain.*

3. *What kind of things do people believe in today that can withstand the kind of argumentation John presents? How do the benefits compare with what John writes?*

DECIDING MY RESPONSE

To think about What specific steps can we take to help people obey the commandment God has given to the church, i.e., love one another, if they are not members? Discuss.

To do This week think of what this lesson means to your faith. Make a decision to share your faith with others and what it means to have eternal life as a result of believing in Him. Then, thank God for His unfailing promise given to those who trust in Him.

WHAT I WILL DO

_____

_____

LIGHT ON THE HEAVY

Trinity—The word Trinity is not found in the Bible and did not find a place formally in the theology of the church until the fourth century. However, it is the distinctive and all comprehensive doctrine of the Christian faith. The Trinity makes three affirmations: that there is but one God; that the Father, the Son and the Spirit is each God; and that the Father, the Son and the Spirit is each a distinct Person.

Although Scripture does not give us a formulated doctrine of the Trinity, it contains all the elements out of which theology has constructed the doctrine. The teachings of Christ bear testimony to the true personality of each of the distinctions within the Godhead and also shed light upon the relations existing between the three Persons. The necessity to formulate the doctrine was thrust upon the church by forces from without; in particular, its faith in the deity of Christ and the necessity to defend it that first compelled the church to formulate a full doctrine of the Trinity for its rule of faith. *(The Interpreter's One Volume Commentary on the Bible,* Abingdon Press, 1971, pp. 1067-1068).

Loyalty and Discipleship

DEFINING THE ISSUE

The 1960's was a turbulent period for Black people. With the rise of the Civil Rights movement, Dr. Martin Luther King, Jr. and many others gathered thousands of people to protest the injustices of the American system. As a result of the marches, demonstrations, and cries for equality, many Blacks lost their lives in the process. Others were threatened, beaten, homes bombed, and they felt the fire of racism from such groups as the Klu Klux Klan and other white supremacists.

Our sense of loyalty and unity was severely tested during this period. For some it was a question of remaining true to the "cause" of equality, while for others, it was a question of survival. Lives were lost in the struggle for equality. But through it all, friendships were bonded and a new era of justice became a reality for Black people.

To be loyal to a cause, a friend, or an institution is one of the hallmarks of the Christian faith. Many people struggle with this issue from time to time. Just as those who faced the racism and hatred of the 1960's had to choose between remaining loyal to the larger goal or giving up in the face of danger, we must also decide where our loyalty will be.

In this lesson the Apostle John continues his exhortation to love one another. He encourages Gaius to be faithful and loyal to brothers and sisters in the Lord regardless of whether they were known or not. This is a lesson we need to learn as we encounter those who are different from us but are still a part of the body of Christ.

AIM

By the end of the study, participants should:

1. Discover what it means to show love by supporting those who share the Gospel.
2. Feel the need of assisting these involved in service to others.
3. Decide to support a minister, missionary or other persons involved in sharing the Gospel of Christ.

SCRIPTURE TEXT

2 JOHN 1 The elder unto the elect lady and her children, whom I love in the truth; and not I only, but also all they that have known the truth;

2 For the truth's sake, which dwelleth in us, and shall be with us for ever.

3 Grace be with you, mercy, and peace, from God the Father, and from the Lord Jesus Christ, the Son of the Father, in truth and love.

4 I rejoiced greatly that I found of thy children walking in truth, as we have received a commandment from the Father.

5 And now I beseech thee, lady, not as though I wrote a new commandment unto thee, but that which we had from the beginning, that we love one another.

6 And this is love, that we walk after his commandments. This is the commandment, that, as ye have heard from the beginning, ye should walk in it.

3 JOHN 1 The elder unto the well-beloved Gaius, whom I love in the truth.

2 Beloved, I wish above all things that thou mayest prosper and be in health, even as thy soul prospereth.

3 For I rejoiced greatly, when the brethren came and testified of the truth that is in thee, even as thou walkest in the truth.

4 I have no greater joy than to hear that my children walk in truth.

5 Beloved, thou doest faithfully whatsoever thou doest to the brethren, and to strangers;

6 Which have borne witness of thy charity before the church: whom if thou bring forward on their journey after a godly sort, thou shalt do well:

7 Because that for His name's sake they went forth, taking nothing of the Gentiles.

8 We therefore ought to receive such, that we might be fellowhelpers to the truth.

BIBLE BACKGROUND

The Apostle John continues his writings in the two shortest books in the Bible, 2 and 3 John. Our study will focus on verses from both books.

In 2 John, the apostle writes to the "elect lady and her children" on the same subject as he had dealt with in 1 John. We are to love one another and walk in Christ's commandments. In 3 John he addresses his letter to "the beloved Gaius", who may have had pastoral responsibilities. John encourages him to be generous to traveling ministers who go forth to proclaim the Word of the Lord. In both cases John's exhortation is meant to help his readers walk in love and truth.

POINTS TO PONDER

1. *To whom did John write 2 John?*
2. *Why did the apostle rejoice?*
3. *How did John want the "elect lady and her children" to walk?*
4. *To whom did John write 3 John?*
5. *Why was John rejoicing at the news about Gaius?*

THE LESSON AT-A-GLANCE

1. *Walking in love (2 John 1-6)*
2. *Walking in truth (3 John:1-4)*
3. *Providing for God's servants (vv. 5-8)*

EXPLORING THE MEANING

1. Walking in love (2 John 1-6)

Letters written in the ancient world usually began by naming the author and then the reader in a formal salutation. In this case, John begins by calling himself "the elder" (v. 1a). The Greek word is *Presbuteros* which may have meant an older man. But in this case, John may have used it to designate a rank or office. Similarly the members of the Sanhedrin council were called *presbuteros;* John had exercised authoritative supervision over a wide circle of churches mentioned in his epistles. So the title could indicate that he was acting in an official capacity.

John addresses his letter to the "elect lady and her children, whom I love in the truth" (v. 1b). Some commentators seem to think that the apostle was writing to a Christian woman of some prominence in the church. According to them the apostle addresses his letter to her and her children, mentions that in his travels he met others of her children, and reports that they were ordering their behavior in the sphere of the truth.

Others seem to think that John was referring to a local church and its members ("her children"). Either way, the apostle loves the lady and her children because of their commitment to the truth. Not only does he love them but many others in the Christian community also love her for the same reason.

After his opening salutation John says, "Grace be with you, mercy, and peace from God the Father; and from the Lord Jesus Christ, the Son of the Father, in truth and love" (v. 3). His greeting is a positive affirmation toward the "lady and her children."

Grace indicates God's unmerited favor freely bestowed on believers, with nothing expected in return. The word "mercy" indicates God's kindness and goodness given to those who deserve condemnation. Peace represents the sum total of the spiritual blessings given to people by God in His grace and mercy. The apostle invokes divine blessings on them from God the Father and from Jesus Christ who provides these blessings for those who belong to Him. For God is truth and love and those who belong to Him practice the same.

The apostle continues his letter by telling "the lady" that he had found some of her children "walking in truth." It could be that a few of her children had decided to follow the commandment John had given to the church earlier (see 1 John 4:21; 5:2). John had come across some of her children, through his preaching and administrative duties, who had conducted themselves by the Word of God. They did not allow outside circumstances to dictate their conduct. Instead, they were following the principles set forth by the Scriptures and this pleased John.

The apostle now gets to the heart of the his letter. He pleads with the lady/church that "we love one another" (v. 5). John makes it clear that he is not writing a new commandment. Instead the apostle used the same words Jesus had given His disciples (John 13:34) over and over. So John is simply recalling how the church members should relate to one another as members of God's family.

2. Walking in truth (3 John 1-4)

Our lesson moves to 3 John where the apostle writes to a specific person ("the well beloved Gaius") about a specific situation. Again John identifies himself as "the elder" who loved Gaius "in the truth."

First, John sends greetings to Gaius. The apostle's hope is that his friend "prosper and be in health," even as his soul prospered (v. 2). There is some possibility that Gaius was not in the best of health and John was invoking physical blessings on him. The verb "prosper" means "to have a good journey" (see Romans 1:10), but in this case it probably means to progress physically as well as one progresses spiritually. What John seems to be saying is that his desire is for Gaius to be blessed—physically, spiritually, and emotionally.

We have the privilege and responsibility as Christians to care for others and to invoke God's blessings on them whenever we can. As we do, the blessings of the Lord will flow in our lives just as freely as we are willing to bless others.

John gives his reason for having confidence in Gaius' spiritual progress. Some Christians ("the brethren") had come to John to report what they knew of him. These brothers were walking in the truth of the Gospel and could see that Gaius was doing the same. This pleased John immensely. One commentator says "the brethren" were probably Christian workers who visited Ephesus on preaching and teaching missions. They would probably report to the apostle what they had learned from various churches on their missions. Gaius may have been one of many workers with whom the apostle was pleased. He concludes this portion of his letter by telling Gaius, "I have no greater joy than to hear that my children walk in truth" (v. 4).

John was happy to know that his spiritual "children" were walking in the truth of the Gospel. None had turned from the truth. The apostle's pastoral leadership may have led many to Jesus Christ and he was pleased that Gaius and his other "children" remained steadfast to the truth they had been taught by him.

3. Providing for God's servants (vv. 5-8)

John is especially pleased about Gaius' faithful service rendered to traveling evangelists and missionaries who had come to the church he was serving. It was also pleasing to know that Gaius was providing shelter and sustenance for "strangers" who visited his church. Gaius had shown brotherly love to others and may have unknowingly entertained angels (see Hebrews 13:1-2).

As a result of Gaius' loving hospitality, the traveling evangelists/missionaries were letting others in the church know of his "love-in-action." Therefore, the apostle asks him to help them continue their journey by providing food, money, housing arrangements, means of travel, or whatever. John's main thought is that Gaius show Christian love and compassion toward those who are God's messengers through his care for them.

John wants Gaius to know that the missionaries/evangelists were totally dependent on God for their support and not on unbelievers ("the Gentiles"). By receiving their support from God's people instead of pagans, the evangelists/missionaries would: (1) bring glory to Jesus' name; and (2) not try to sell the Gospel cheaply to unbelievers in order to support themselves.

Gaius' financial/material support for the evangelists/missionaries would actually make him a co-laborer ("fellow workers") with them. His unselfish action made him a part of their work because of his willingness to give to others who were preaching the Gospel.

We are reminded that we, too, should work to spread the Gospel wherever we can. Some of us may not have the opportunity to go to Africa or other continents where God's Word is needed. But we can support missionaries and evangelists with our financial help and through prayer. As we do God will bless us and continue to provide for our needs because of our willingness to be a blessing to others.

DISCERNING MY DUTY

1. *Why is it so important that we live according to God's commandments?*
2. *What does it mean to "walk in the truth"?*
3. *Discuss what it means to be a "fellow-helper" with missionaries/evangelists.*

DECIDING MY RESPONSE

To think about—Given today's economic conditions is it

always expedient to financially support missionaries/evangelists who are working in other countries? What steps can Christians take to see that money given for missions and evangelism does not end up in the wrong person's pocket? Discuss.

To do—This week reflect on your life as a "fellow worker" of the Gospel. Are you supportive of the work of others? If not, find a ministry to which you can lend time or finances this week. Be prepared to give a praise report to the class next week.

WHAT I WILL DO

_____

_____

LIGHT ON THE HEAVY

Church—The English "church" derives from the Greek word Kuriakos ("belonging to the Lord"), and it stands for another Greek word *Ekklesia* (where we get the word "ecclesiastical"), denoting an assembly.

In the Gospels the term is found only in Matthew 16:18 and 18:17. From the outset the Church has both a local and a general significance, denoting both the individual assembly and the worldwide community. However there is no tension between the local and the universal sense. Each church or congregation is the Church in its own setting, and each a manifestation or concretion of the whole church. This means that there is scope for great flexibility in organization and structure according to particular and varying needs. At the worldwide level, it is unlikely that there can ever be more than the loosest practical interconnection. Varying degrees of integration are possible at national, provincial or municipal levels. But the basic unity is always the local church, not in isolation or as a parochially-minded body, but as a congregation of the universal fellowship with a strong sense of belonging to it. *(The Zondervan Bible Dictionary,* 1962, pp. 170-171.)